SHORT NON-FICTION

MATTERS OF FACT

BRIAN KELLOW

JOHN KRISAK

PRENTICE-HALL CANADA INC.

SCARBOROUGH, ONTARIO

Canadian Cataloguing in Publication Data
Main entry under title:

Matters of fact : short non-fiction

Includes index.
ISBN 0-13-560871-6

1. Readers (Secondary). 2. Canadian prose
literature (English).* 3. American prose
literature. I. Kellow, Brian. II. Krisak, John.

PE1121.K45 1992   C818'.08   C91-094144-0

ISBN 0-13-560871-6

Prentice-Hall, Inc., Englewood Cliffs, New Jersey
Prentice-Hall International, Inc., London
Prentice-Hall of Australia, Pty., Ltd., Sydney
Prentice-Hall of India Pvt., Ltd., New Delhi
Prentice-Hall of Japan, Inc., Tokyo
Prentice-Hall of Southeast Asia (PTE) Ltd., Singapore
Editora Prentice-Hall do Brasil Ltda., Rio de Janeiro
Prentice-Hall Hispanoamericana, S.A., Mexico

ISBN 0-13-560871-6

Research and Marketing Manager: *David Steele*
Managing Editor: *Alan Simpson*
Editors: *Linda Bishop, Chelsea Donaldson*
Production Coordinator: *Crystale Chalmers*
Art Director: *Gail Ferreira Ng-A-Kien*
Design: *Holly Fisher & Associates*
Cover Art: *Christopher Griffin*
Permissions: *Sharon Houston, Dorothy Melly*
Composition and Typesetting: *Computer Composition of Canada Inc.*

Printed and bound in Canada by Webcom Limited
1 2 3 4 5 6 W 97 96 95 94 93 92

Policy Statement
Prentice-Hall Canada Inc., School Division, and the editors of *Matters of Fact: Short Non-fiction* are committed to the publication of instructional materials that are as bias-free as possible. This anthology was evaluated for bias prior to publication.

The editors and publisher also recognize the importance of appropriate reading levels and have therefore made every effort to ensure the highest degree of readability in the anthology. The content has been selected and organized at a level suitable to the intended audience.

Research indicates that readability is affected by much more than word or sentence length; factors such as presentation, format, and design, none of which are considered in the usual readability tests, also greatly influence the ease with which students read a book. These and many additional features have been carefully prepared to ensure maximum student comprehension.

Contents

Acknowledgements

This project has been enriched by the support of many people — colleagues, friends and family whose help we would now like to formally acknowledge. Special thanks are also extended to the following people at Prentice-Hall Canada Inc. whose contributions to this book have been extensive and with whom we have worked so closely — David Steele, Alan Simpson, Linda Bishop, Chelsea Donaldson, and Crystale Chalmers.

John Krisak
Brian Kellow

For Jane and Leah, Peggy and Cyril

Prentice-Hall Canada Inc. wishes to express its sincere appreciation to the following Canadian educators for contributing their time and expertise during the development of this anthology.

John Borovilos, Head of English, Danforth Collegiate and Technical Institute, Toronto, Ontario

Stephen D. Bailey, English Department Head, Burnaby North Secondary School, Burnaby School District, Burnaby, B.C.

Mark Brubacher, Consultant for Student-Centred Learning, Board of Education for the City of York, Ontario

Marian R. Hood, Dr. E.P. Scarlett High School, Calgary Board of Education, Calgary, Alberta

Jill Kedersha McClay, University of Alberta, Edmonton, Alberta

Bob Pembroke, English Department Head, Dartmouth High School, Dartmouth District, Dartmouth, Nova Scotia

Peter Prest, Assistant Principal, John S. Diefenbaker High School, Calgary Board of Education, Calgary, Alberta

Gail C. Roberts, English Language Arts Coordinator (Secondary), St. James Assiniboia School Division #2, Winnipeg, Manitoba

Inclusion of a person in this list does not necessarily indicate endorsement of the text.

ONE ANOTHER

BEAUTY: WHEN THE OTHER DANCER IS THE SELF

ALICE WALKER

- In your journal, describe those things about yourself which you have the most difficulty accepting.
- How is your position in your family different from that of other family members?

I t is a bright summer day in 1947. My father, a fat, funny man with beautiful eyes and a subversive wit, is trying to decide which of his eight children he will take with him to the county fair. My mother, of course, will not go. She is knocked out from getting most of us ready: I hold my neck still against the pressure of her knuckles as she hastily completes the braiding and then beribboning of my hair.

My father is the driver for the rich old white lady up the road. Her name is Miss Mey. She owns all the land for miles around, as well as the house in which we live. All I remember about her is that she once offered to pay my mother thirty-five cents for cleaning her house, raking up piles of her magnolia leaves, and washing her family's clothes, and that my mother — she of no money, eight children, and a chronic earache — refused it. But I do not think of this in 1947. I am two and a half years old. I want to go everywhere my daddy goes. I am excited at the prospect of riding in a car. Someone has told me fairs are fun. That there is room in the car for only three of us doesn't faze me at all. Whirling happily in my starchy frock, showing off my biscuit-polished patent-leather shoes and lavender socks, tossing my head in a way that makes my ribbons bounce, I stand, hands on hips, before my father. "Take me, Daddy," I say with assurance; "I'm the prettiest!"

Later, it does not surprise me to find myself in Miss Mey's shiny black car, sharing the back seat with the other lucky ones. Does not surprise me that I thoroughly enjoy the fair. At home that night I tell the unlucky ones all I can remember about the merry-go-round, the man who eats live chickens, and the teddy bears, until they say: that's enough, baby Alice. Shut up now, and go to sleep.

It is Easter Sunday, 1950. I am dressed in a green, flocked, scalloped-hem dress (handmade by my adoring sister, Ruth) that has its own smooth satin petticoat and tiny hot-pink roses tucked into each scallop. My shoes, new T-strap patent leather, again highly biscuit-polished. I am six years old and have learned one of the longest Easter speeches to be heard that day, totally unlike the speech I said when I was two: "Easter lilies / pure and white / blossom in / the morning light." When I rise to give my speech I do so on a great wave of love and pride and expectation. People in the church stop rustling their new crinolines. They seem to hold their breath. I can tell they admire my dress, but it is my spirit, bordering on sassiness (womanishness), they secretly applaud.

"That girl's a little *mess*," they whisper to each other, pleased.

Naturally I say my speech without stammer or pause, unlike those who stutter, stammer, or, worst of all, forget. This is before the word "beautiful" exists in people's vocabulary, but "Oh, isn't she the *cutest* thing!" frequently floats my way. "And got so much sense!" they gratefully add . . . for which thoughtful addition I thank them to this day.

It was great fun being cute. But then, one day, it ended.

I am eight years old and a tomboy. I have a cowboy hat, cowboy boots, checkered shirt and pants, all red. My playmates are my brothers, two and four years older than I. Their colors are black and green, the only difference in the way we are dressed. On Saturday nights we all go to the picture show, even my mother; Westerns are her favorite kind of movie. Back home, "on the ranch," we pretend we are Tom Mix, Hopalong Cassidy, Lash LaRue (we've even named one of our dogs Lash LaRue); we chase each other for hours rustling cattle, being outlaws, delivering damsels from distress. Then my parents decide to buy my brothers guns. These are not "real" guns. They shoot "BBs," copper pellets my brothers say will kill birds. Because I am a girl, I do not get a gun. Instantly I am relegated to the position of Indian. Now there appears a great distance between us. They shoot and shoot at everything with their new guns. I try to keep up with my bow and arrows.

One day while I am standing on top of our makeshift "garage" — pieces of tin nailed across some poles — holding my bow and arrow and looking out toward the fields, I feel an incredible blow in my right eye. I look down just in time to see my brother lower his gun.

Both brothers rush to my side. My eye stings, and I cover it with my hand. "If you tell," they say, "we will get a whipping. You don't want that to happen, do you?" I do not. "Here is a piece of wire," says the older brother, picking it up from the roof; "say you stepped on one end of it and the other flew up and hit you." The pain is beginning to start. "Yes," I say. "Yes, I will say that is what happened." If I do not say this is what happened, I know my brothers will find ways to make me wish I had. But now I will say anything that gets me to my mother.

Confronted by our parents we stick to the lie agreed upon. They place me on a bench on the porch and I close my left eye while they examine the right. There is a tree growing from underneath the porch that climbs past the railing to the roof. It is the last thing my right eye sees. I watch as its trunk, its branches, and then its leaves are blotted out by the rising blood.

I am in shock. First there is intense fever, which my father tries to break using lily leaves bound around my head. Then there are chills: my mother tries to get me to eat soup. Eventually, I do not know how, my parents learn what has happened. A week after the "accident" they take me to see a doctor. "Why did you wait so long to come?" he asks, looking into my eye and shaking his head. "Eyes are sympathetic," he says. "If one is blind, the other will likely become blind too."

This comment of the doctor's terrifies me. But it is really how I look that bothers me most. Where the BB pellet struck there is a glob of whitish scar tissue, a hideous cataract, on my eye. Now when I stare at people — a favorite pastime, up to now — they will stare back. Not at the "cute" little girl, but at her scar. For six years I do not stare at anyone, because I do not raise my head.

Years later, in the throes of a mid-life crisis, I ask my mother and sister whether I changed after the "accident." "No," they say, puzzled. "What do you mean?"

What do I mean?

I am eight, and, for the first time, doing poorly in school, where I have been something of a whiz since I was four. We have just moved to the place where the "accident" occurred. We do not know any of the people around us because this is a different county. The only time I see the friends I knew is when we go back to our old church. The new school is the former state penitentiary. It is a large stone building, cold and drafty, crammed to overflowing with boisterous, ill-disciplined children. On the third floor there is a huge circular imprint of some partition that has been torn out.

"What used to be here?" I ask a sullen girl next to me on our way past it to lunch.

"The electric chair," says she.

At night I have nightmares about the electric chair, and about all the people reputedly "fried" in it. I am afraid of the school, where all the students seem to be budding criminals.

"What's the matter with your eye?" they ask, critically.

When I don't answer (I cannot decide whether it was an "accident" or not), they shove me, insist on a fight.

My brother, the one who created the story about the wire, comes to my rescue. But then brags so much about "protecting" me, I become sick.

After months of torture at the school, my parents decide to send me back to our old community, to my old school. I live with my grandparents and the teacher they board. But there is no room for Phoebe, my cat. By the time my grandparents decide there *is* room, and I ask for my cat, she cannot be found. Miss Yarborough, the boarding teacher, takes me under her wing, and begins to teach me to play the piano. But soon she marries an African — a "prince," she says — and is whisked away to his continent.

At my old school there is at least one teacher who loves me. She is the teacher who "knew me before I was born" and bought my first baby clothes. It is she who makes life bearable. It is her presence that finally helps me turn on the one child at the school who continually calls me "one-eyed bitch." One day I simply grab him by his coat and beat him until I am satisfied. It is my teacher who tells me my mother is ill.

My mother is lying in bed in the middle of the day, something I have never seen. She is in too much pain to speak. She has an abscess in her ear. I stand looking down on her, knowing that if she dies, I cannot live. She is being treated with warm oils and hot bricks held against her cheek. Finally a doctor comes. But I must go back to my grandparents' house. The weeks pass but I am hardly aware of it. All I know is that my mother might die, my father is not so jolly, my brothers still have their guns, and I am the one sent away from home.

"You did not change," they say.

Did I imagine the anguish of never looking up?

I am twelve. When relatives come to visit I hide in my room. My cousin Brenda, just my age, whose father works in the post office and whose mother is a nurse, comes to find me. "Hello," she says. And then she asks, looking at my recent school picture, which I did not want taken, and on which the "glob," as I think of it, is clearly visible, "You still can't see out of that eye?"

"No," I say, and flop back on the bed over my book.

That night, as I do almost every night, I abuse my eye. I rant and rave at it, in front of the mirror. I plead with it to clear up before morning. I tell it I hate and despise it. I do not pray for sight. I pray for beauty.

"You did not change," they say.

I am fourteen and baby-sitting for my brother Bill, who lives in Boston. He is my favorite brother and there is a strong bond between us. Understanding my feelings of shame and ugliness he and his wife take me to a local hospital, where the "glob" is removed by a doctor named O. Henry. There is still a small bluish crater where the scar tissue was, but the ugly white stuff is gone. Almost immediately I become a different person from the girl who does not raise her head. Or so I think. Now that I've raised my head I win the boyfriend of my dreams. Now that I've raised my head I have plenty of friends. Now that I've raised my head classwork comes from my lips as faultlessly as Easter speeches did, and I leave high school as valedictorian, most popular student, and *queen*, hardly believing my luck. Ironically, the girl who was voted most beautiful in our class (and was) was later shot twice through the chest by a male companion, using a "real" gun, while she was pregnant. But that's another story in itself. Or is it?

"You did not change," they say.

It is now thirty years since the "accident." A beautiful journalist comes to visit and to interview me. She is going to write a cover story for her magazine that focuses on my latest book. "Decide how you want to look on the cover," she says. "Glamorous, or whatever."

Never mind, "glamorous," it is the "whatever" that I hear. Suddenly all I can think of is whether I will get enough sleep the night before the photography session: if I don't my eye will be tired and wander, as blind eyes will.

At night in bed with my lover I think up reasons why I should not appear on the cover of a magazine. "My meanest critics will say I've sold out," I say. "My family will now realize I write scandalous books."

"But what's the real reason you don't want to do this?" he asks.

"Because in all probability," I say in a rush, "my eye won't be straight."

"It will be straight enough," he says. Then, "Besides, I thought you'd made your peace with that."

And I suddenly remember that I have.

I remember:

I am talking to my brother Jimmy, asking if he remembers anything unusual about the day I was shot. He does not know I consider that day the last time my father, with his sweet home remedy of cool lily leaves, chose me, and that I suffered and raged inside because of this. "Well," he says, "all I remember is standing by the side of the highway with Daddy, trying to flag down a car. A white man stopped, but when Daddy said he needed somebody to take his little girl to the doctor, he drove off."

I remember:

I am in the desert for the first time. I fall totally in love with it. I am so overwhelmed by its beauty, I confront for the first time, consciously, the meaning of the doctor's words years ago: "Eyes are sympathetic. If one is blind, the other will likely become blind too." I realize I have dashed about the world madly, looking at this, looking at that, storing up images against the fading of the light. *But I might have missed seeing the desert!* The shock of that possibility — and gratitude for over twenty-five years of sight — sends me literally to my knees. Poem after poem comes — which is perhaps how poets pray.

On Sight

I am so thankful I have seen
The Desert
And the creatures in the desert
And the desert itself.

The desert has its own moon
Which I have seen
With my own eye.

There is no flag on it.

Trees of the desert have arms
All of which are always up
That is because the moon is up
The sun is up
Also the sky
The stars
Clouds
None with flags.

If there *were* flags, I doubt
The trees would point.
Would you?

But mostly, I remember this:

I am twenty-seven, and my baby daughter is almost three. Since her birth I have worried about her discovery that her mother's eyes are different from other people's. Will she be embarrassed? I think. What will she say? Every day she watches a television program called "Big Blue Marble." It begins with a picture of the earth as it appears from the moon. It is bluish, a little battered-looking, but full of light, with whitish clouds swirling around it. Every time I see it I weep with love, as if it is a picture of Grandma's house. One day when I am putting Rebecca down for her nap, she suddenly focuses on my eye. Something inside me cringes, gets ready to try to protect myself. All children are cruel about physical differences, I know from experience, and that they don't always mean to be is another matter. I assume Rebecca will be the same.

But no-o-o-o. She studies my face intently as we stand, her inside and me outside her crib. She even holds my face maternally between her dimpled little hands. Then, looking every bit as serious and lawyerlike as her father, she says, as if it may just possibly have slipped my attention: "Mommy, there's a *world* in your eye." (As in, "Don't be alarmed, or do anything crazy.") And then, gently, but with great interest: "Mommy, where did you *get* that world in your eye?"

For the most part, the pain left then. (So what, if my brothers grew up to buy even more powerful pellet guns for their sons and to carry real guns themselves. So what, if a young "Morehouse man" once nearly fell off the steps of Trevor Arnett Library because he thought my eyes were blue.) Crying and laughing I ran to the bathroom, while Rebecca mumbled and sang herself off to sleep. Yes indeed, I realized, looking into the mirror. There *was* a world in my eye. And I saw that it was possible to love it: that in fact, for all it had taught me of shame and anger and inner vision, I *did* love it. Even to see it drifting out of orbit in boredom, or rolling up out of fatigue, not to mention floating back at attention in excitement (bearing witness, a friend has called it), deeply suitable to my personality, and even characteristic of me.

That night I dream I am dancing to Stevie Wonder's song "Always" (the name of the song is really, "As," but I hear it as "Always"). As I dance, whirling and joyous, happier than I've ever been in my life, another bright-faced dancer joins me. We dance and kiss each other and hold each other through the night. The other dancer has obviously come through all right, as I have done. She is beautiful, whole and free. And she is also me.

RESPONSE

1. With which aspects of Walker's childhood do you identify? Why?
2. Do you think that Walker was oversensitive about her appearance? Explain.
3. "There *was* a world in my eye. And I saw that it was possible to love it: that in fact for all it had taught me of shame and anger and inner vision, I *did* love it."
   a) What do you think the author means with these two sentences?
   b) Explain how the writer came to this realization about herself.

EXTENSION

4. a) Identify six incidents from your own life. Write a paragraph about each incident. Look for a common thread through each of these incidents.
   b) What can you learn about yourself from this process?

GIANTS, WIZARDS, AND DWARFS

ROBERT FULGHUM

- What was your favourite childhood game? Why?
- In your journal, recount an incident from elementary school in which you were labelled by your teachers or your classmates.

G iants, wizards, and dwarfs was the game to play.
Being left in charge of about eighty children seven to ten years old, while their parents were off doing parenty things, I mustered my troops in the church social hall and explained the game. It's a large-scale version of Rock, Paper, and Scissors, and involves some intellectual decision making. But the real purpose of the game is to make a lot of noise and run around chasing people until nobody knows which side you are on or who won.

Organizing a roomful of wired-up gradeschoolers into two teams, explaining the rudiments of the game, achieving consensus on group identity — all this is no mean accomplishment, but we did it with a right good will and were ready to go.

The excitement of the chase had reached a critical mass. I yelled out: "You have to decide *now* which you are — a GIANT, a WIZARD, or a DWARF!"

While the groups huddled in frenzied, whispered consultation, a tug came at my pants leg. A small child stands there looking up, and asks in a small, concerned voice, "Where do the Mermaids stand?"

Where do the Mermaids stand?

A long pause. A *very* long pause. "Where do the Mermaids stand?" says I.

"Yes. You see, I am a Mermaid."

"There are no such things as Mermaids."

"Oh, yes, I am one!"

She did not relate to being a Giant, a Wizard, or a Dwarf. She knew her category. Mermaid. And was not about to leave the game and go over and stand against the wall where a loser would stand. She intended to participate, wherever Mermaids fit into the scheme of things. Without giving up dignity or identity. She took it for granted that there was a place for Mermaids and that I would know just where.

Well, where DO the Mermaids stand? All the "Mermaids" — all those who are different, who do not fit the norm and who do not accept the available boxes and pigeonholes?

Answer that question and you can build a school, a nation, or a world on it.

What was my answer at the moment? Every once in a while I say the right thing. "The Mermaid stands right here by the King of the Sea!" says I. (*Yes, right here by the King's Fool, I thought to myself.*)

So we stood there hand in hand, reviewing the troops of Wizards and Giants and Dwarfs as they roiled by in wild disarray.

It is not true, by the way, that mermaids do not exist. I know at least one personally. I have held her hand.

RESPONSE

1. What is the point in a game in which "nobody knows which side you are on or who won"?
2. From the point of view of the small child, what does it mean to be a "mermaid"?
3. What becomes of the people "who do not accept the available boxes and pigeonholes"?

4. With your group, devise a scheme for a school in which everyone learns and no one loses. Invite the principal to your class to listen and respond to your schemes.

SELF-RESPECT

G. KINGSLEY WARD

- What do you understand by the expression "self-respect"?
- Do you think there is a difference between self-respect and "reputation"? Explain.

My Disillusioned Daughter:

What a letdown it was, hearing that the big party you had so looked forward to last Saturday was a disaster and a source of great embarrassment for several of your young friends, most especially for one of your closest friends. Having a good time is one thing, having a good time that demeans oneself and offends others is quite a different matter. Obviously, your friend's joviality lapsed into the second category.

I take it she got totally carried away and performed some pretty unusual antics of which she is now highly ashamed. As you say, perhaps she had just tried too hard to be the hit of the party and it boomeranged on her at a terrible cost: the loss of her all-round respect. But a moment's stupidity often backfires that way, causing us days, weeks, or even months of feeling shame and self-reproach.

Needless to say, I am extremely happy and proud (and thankful!) that you survived this party with no distortion of your fine image. I hope you will always continue to hold firm your own self-respect and the respect of all who know you, for it is probably the most valuable jewel of life.

Having people respect you means that you are being held in high regard for your moral values. It goes without saying that it is difficult to respect a thief, a prostitute, an alcoholic, a drug user, or anyone who abuses or corrupts either themselves or others in the pursuit of money, power, or so-called fun. But such extremes aside, it seems to me that maintaining one's self-respect and that of others while going through youthful years is a particularly hazardous affair.

It is only human to want to have friends and to feel accepted and liked by other people — a desire that is more pronounced in youth than in later years. Particularly among the young there is all too often one unfortunate person who is refused acceptance by "the crowd" because of a lack of personality (which has probably not yet even fully developed), or a lack of attractiveness, or a lack of some kind of sports or arts ability. In short, such a person appears to own none of the attributes that normally attract one person to another or that cause other people to want to be in his company. This can be dangerous for the outcast for, in his overzealous pursuit of friendship and in his desire to become "one of the gang," he often starts behaving as he thinks others want him to behave and not at all according to his own finer instincts. He drinks to excess, and/or gets hooked on drugs, and/or steals (if not for money, for the "adventure"), and/or abuses people, sometimes sexually, to prove either his cool worldliness or his physical strength. Inevitably, one morning, he wakes up wondering where his self-esteem went and when it left.

I do not believe that youthful years are any more perilous now than they have ever been, but there is no doubt that they are and always have been the most treacherously challenging of all. Fortunately, many of the hazards of these years almost magically start disintegrating as maturity and the assumption of adult responsibilities begin. Until this natural transition occurs, however, it would be prudent to heed the admonition of Marcus Aurelius Antonius of about 160 A.D.: "Never esteem anything as of advantage to you that shall make you break your word or lose your self-respect."

Unnerved by your friend's shocking behaviour, you stated that you never want to find yourself in a similar position and asked how you can make sure that you never do. Well, for one thing, it takes some thinking *beforehand*. For a start, travel with a group of friends who, like you, wish to avoid any activities that might bring disrespect to themselves or to their families. If that is hard to accomplish, then finding even one good friend who is of strong moral fibre is a great help. It is a big world out there and facing it all by yourself on some occasions can be a lonely battle. You will learn to confront it alone in time, but during these growing years, you can do with a little moral support now and then. As one voice in a crowd, you feel as ineffectual as a mouse but, although one friend and you equals only two, that second person's support is often worth the strength of an army. The same, of course, applies the other way — when your friend might need backup for his or her point of view.

Another good, precautionary method of avoiding disgraceful behaviour is to imagine the personal hurt it would inflict upon your family. Aside from bringing dismay or embarrassment or even financial expenses down on their heads to bail you out of some legal predicament, think of the agony involved — theirs and yours — in their losing respect for you. There are consequences to every action; some thought given to them beforehand is a great protector of self-esteem.

Because your self-respect and conscience would suffer if you did not, try to help your friend now that she is in trouble. Now is the time to go to her and prove to her that you are a true friend in tough times as well as in good. It builds character to help another in times of trouble — especially in such as this, which presents the opportunity of trying to shield her from repeating her mistake on future occasions. A word of caution, though: gauge your friend's progress and decide whether she is sincerely trying to clean up her act. Some people learn nothing from their mistakes, and any effort to help them is as futile as trying to stop Niagara Falls from falling. By your friend's future behaviour, you will have to judge whether she is or is not deserving of your continued friendship and allegiance. Some people are not. And I re-emphasize that your best method of warding off unnecessary trouble is by being discerning in your selection of friends.

I should like to think that I have taught you well about handling alcohol with care; that if it is used, it should be only for relaxation or fun and never in courting disaster. And you know my feelings about drugs — that if there must be a choice between drugs or alcohol, you would be much better off to stick to alcohol. It has one main ingredient, ethyl alcohol, and your body is geared to throw off its effects, even those of over-consumption, within twenty-four hours. Human beings have had a lot of experience with alcohol and its effects on the body, so we know what we are dealing with here. Not so with drugs. The use of drugs is still a fairly recent development within our society and the effects of the many chemical combinations in drugs, both hard and soft, on the human system have yet to be determined. Marijuana alone contains over four hundred separate chemical properties, some of which remain in the body for a long time. The long-term effects of many such drugs, because of their multi-facet make-up, is still a profoundly disconcerting unknown. An alcoholic's chances of resuming normal bodily health once he stops imbibing liquor are usually quite good. That is a known. But only time can yet prove what a drug abuser's long-term health prospects are once he kicks his lethal habit. Scary, scary business!

And don't for a moment believe as some do, that the avoidance of a hangover is some special advantage of taking certain drugs over alcohol. It is a foolish and dangerous delusion. A hangover is your body's built-in policing system telling you that you had too much to drink the night before. Of what advantage are no warning signals that you smoked or snorted or shot up too much the night before?

Enjoy your parties but, I repeat, if you must choose between booze or drugs, stick to booze. Not only is it the less potential hazard to your health of the two, it is legal to consume. (But if you do drink at parties, be sure to give me a call for a lift home.)

The sex scene is another area fraught with potential dangers. When the Good Lord made us, He included sexual drive among all the other many good things with which He endowed us. At times, however, I am sure that many feel He almost overcharged our bodies with sexual desire — why else is it so hard on some occasions to curb our emotions so that they do not override our moral standards? Hard it is at times, but I can assure you that the extra effort on those occasions is worth the mighty reward of feeling proud of the strength of your convictions. Again, the consequences of all our actions and how we feel about our-selves — good or bad in their wake — is, I believe, what matters most in this department, just as it does in all other areas of our lives. Self-respect cannot exclude respect for our bodies.

This letter could go on forever on the topic of self-respect and the sundry ways it can be squandered, shattered, or battered. Far more important, is that its value be esteemed and regarded as vital to our well-being as is the air we breathe. Living without it is hardly living at all.

Robert Louis Stevenson said. "Youth is wholly experimental." Please pick your experiments carefully and perspicaciously. (And yes, you might have to look up that last word in your dictionary.)

Love, Daddy

RESPONSE

1. What do you think of the following words of advice which this man gives his daughter?
   a) " . . . it seems to me that maintaining one's self-respect and that of others while going through youthful years is a particularly hazardous affair."
   b) " . . . in his desire to become 'one of the gang,' he often starts behaving as he thinks others want him to behave and not at all according to his own finer instincts."
   c) 'Never esteem anything as of advantage to you that shall make you break your word or lose your self-respect.'
   d) "Self-respect cannot exclude respect for our bodies."

EXTENSION

2. Write a letter to someone known to you who is in danger of losing his or her self-respect.
3. In groups, compose a "list of rules" which will enable you to maintain your self-respect throughout your life.

THE DAY DAD MADE TOAST

SARAH DURKEE

- Who prepares most of the meals in your household?
- Are there special occasions when someone else prepares the meals?
- Who looks after the "emergencies" in your household?
- Who manages the various medical/dental and other appointments in your household?

I 'll never forget the day Dad made toast. It was a sunny Saturday morning in late October near Halloween. I remember it was Halloween because Mom was outside putting a scarecrow with a pumpkin head up on the roof. Dad was in bed.

"Hey kids!" he hollered from their bedroom. "C'mere!"

My older sister Lucy and little brother Danny and I were busy watching the Three Stooges, but we ran upstairs during the commercial. Dad sprang out of bed in his underwear like a ringmaster.

"Here they are!" he bellowed joyfully. "My *kids*!! The greatest kids in the *world*!" He grabbed us to his chest and squished our faces together. This wasn't at all like him. Something was up. "Where's your beautiful mother?!"

"Out on the roof," Lucy said.

He pulled us over to the window that looked out onto the roof. My mom was out there in her ripped overalls with a bunch of tools sticking out of her pockets. She had finished setting up the pumpkin man and was now fixing the TV antenna. Dad tapped on the window.

"LINDA!" he shouted. "COME ON IN, HONEY!"

Mom looked up cheerfully. She had nails in her mouth.

"JUSHT A SHECUND!" she yelled. "I SHEE A LOOSH SHINGLE!"

Clutching her hammer, she scrambled toward the shingle on all fours.

Dad grinned down at us.

"Should I tell her?" he asked.

Mom's hammering rang through the house.

"Tell her *what*?? What's going *on*??"

"Well . . ." Dad smiled, and then he broke the big news. "I'M GOING TO MAKE TOAST!!"

"WOW!" we cried. "*Really*, Dad?? *Today*??"

"Yup!" he beamed proudly. "Right this minute! And we're not talking ordinary ho-hum *toast*, believe you me . . . we're talking Dad's special *cinnamon* toast!! And I don't want your mom to lift a *finger*, I'm handling the *whole thing*!"

"Oooooh!"

He tapped on the window again. "LINDA!" he yelled. "MEET US IN THE KITCHEN! I HAVE A SURPRISE FOR YOU!"

"OKAY, SWEETHEART!" Mom shouted as she hung from a ladder, clearing leaves from the gutter. "I'LL BE RIGHT DOWN!"

Lucy and Danny and I sat on the end of the bed, waiting for further instructions. We love it when he gets in these moods. One time he decided we should cook Thanksgiving dinner on the outdoor grill. It tasted weird. Another time he decided the whole family was getting flabby, and we started doing calisthenics out in the yard every morning. On the third day he twisted his ankle, so we stopped.

Dad went over to the chair where he always throws his clothes at night and pulled on his jeans. "Okay, kids, listen up!" he said. "Your mother and I both work really hard all week. I figure the least I can do . . ."

Mom started hammering something again.

"I FIGURE THE LEAST I CAN DO," he shouted over the banging, "IS TAKE SOME OF THE HOUSEWORK LOAD OFF HER ONCE IN A WHILE! WE'VE ALL GOT TO LEND A HAND! PITCH IN! DO OUR BIT! SHE'LL REALLY APPRECIATE IT!"

The hammering stopped. Dad pulled on a T-shirt that says "Are we having fun yet?" and jabbed his fist in the air like a football coach.

"Let's hit that kitchen, team!"

We raced him downstairs.

The kitchen was still pretty neat from the night before. We all kind of wandered around for a second not quite knowing how to start. Dad opened and closed a few cabinets. "Now let's see . . ." he muttered. "*Plates* . . . . where do we keep the ones I like . . . y'know, those big blue plates we have? . . ."

Mom knocked on the kitchen door with her elbow. She was lugging two pots of geraniums. Dad flung open the door and gave her a kiss.

"Thanks!" Mom said as she passed through to the living room. "It's about time I brought these indoors!"

Dad sort of jogged along behind her to the doorway. "Breakfast is coming right up, angelface! I'm making my special *cinnamon* toast! Just leave everything to me! You're gonna *love* it!"

Mom's voice drifted back from the family room. "Terrific, hon!"

"Um . . . Linda?" he called. "Where are the big blue plates?"

"In the dishwasher!" Mom yelled.

Dad snapped his fingers. "RIGHT!"

Danny and I got the plates and juice glasses from the dishwasher and started to put them on the table. Mom came back in dragging the vacuum cleaner behind her. She picked up the phone and called her office.

"No, no, kids!" said Dad. "The plates have to be *preheated!* That's what they do in fancy restaurants. It makes the toast stay warm longer!" He grabbed the plates, put them in the oven, and turned away.

"Oh," we said. We turned the oven on. Dad's very absent-minded.

"Hi, it's me," Mom said on the phone. "I spoke to the Blums and they're willing to go to seventy-three-five. They'd like to pass papers on Thursday."

Mom's a real estate agent. They all talk like that.

She hung up the phone, plugged in the vacuum, and rounded the corner to the dining room accompanied by a whir so deafening that we all had to shout.

"OKAY," Dad yelled. "LET'S GET THIS SHOW ON THE ROAD! JENNY," — that's me — "WE NEED ABOUT A DOZEN SLICES OF BREAD! *WHITE* BREAD, NOT THE HEALTHY KIND.''

"BUT MOM LIKES US TO USE THE HEALTHY KIND!" I reminded him.

"JUST THIS *ONCE*! THIS IS 'DAD'S SPECIAL TOAST'! HEALTHY BREAD DOESN'T WORK! NOW WHERE'S THAT DARN TOASTER?!''

"HERE, DAD," Danny giggled. It had a quilted toaster cover over it.

"NOW WHY WOULD ANYBODY WANT TO COVER UP A TOASTER?!'' Dad grumbled.

Lucy and I tried not to laugh but Danny was too young to know any better.

"DADDY COULDN'T FIND THE *TOASTER*!" he shrieked. "HEEE HEEE HEE HA HA HA!!''

"I *KNOW* WHERE THE *TOASTER* IS, DANNY, I JUST COULDN'T *SEE* IT! NOW GET OVER THERE AND HELP JENNY COUNT THE BREAD.''

The vacuuming stopped. Mom walked through on her way down to the laundry room with a huge armload of dirty clothes.

"Uh, Linda?" Dad said brightly with his head in a cupboard. "Sugar?''

"Yes, cupcake?" she answered.

"No, honey, I mean *where's the sugar*," said Dad. "I don't see it in here.''

"Bottom shelf!" yelled Mom on her way to the basement.

"RIGHT!" yelled Dad, spotting the sugar bag. "Okay, kids! Start toasting that bread! Lucy, you and I will make the cinnamon mixture. Let's see . . . cinnamon . . . sugar . . .''

"How about a bowl to mix it in?" said Lucy, handing him a bowl.

"RIGHT!" said Dad. "Now watch closely." He started spooning sugar and shaking cinnamon. "*Equal parts* of each. That's the real secret to this. A lot of people skimp on the cinnamon.''

Mom started a buzz saw in the basement. She's been building new shelves for the family room. Also a sun deck. Also an addition to the garage.

"How's that first batch of toast coming, guys?" Dad called to Danny and me.

"Okay," I said. "What should we do when it's done?"

Mom came up from the basement tugging a bag of cement mix. "Bulkhead's stuck shut," she said. "I better go out and pry it open."

"Butter it and bring it over to me and Lucy *fast*," Dad said. "We'll sprinkle it with the cinnamon mixture and then whisk each batch into the oven with the preheated plates."

Mom muscled the cement mix out the kitchen door.

"There's orange juice in the fridge," she called over her shoulder.

"Don't you budge, sweetie!" Dad called after her. "I'll take care of it!"

Danny poured the juice and put napkins on the table. I kept buttering the toast when it popped up and IMMEDIATELY brought it to Dad who IMMEDIATELY sprinkled it with the cinnamon mixture and gave it to Lucy who IMMEDIATELY put it in the oven with the preheated plates. Once we'd gotten our system down pat, Dad relaxed a little.

"Y'know, kids," he mused, "times have really changed. I mean my father wouldn't have been caught *dead* doing any housework. It just wasn't something men *did*; it was women's work. But we're modern families now, and here you have a manly guy like me pitching in like this after a hard week's work — making breakfast so his wife can take a little break. It's beautiful, isn't it?"

"It's beautiful, Dad."

"We've really come a long way," he said.

"We really have, Dad."

Just as Lucy was putting the last piece of toast in the oven, Mom knocked on the door with her elbow again. "COULD SOMEBODY OPEN THE DOOR, PLEASE?"

Dad rushed over to let her in.

"Thanks. My hands are *filthy*! I didn't even want to touch the doorknob!"

"Ready for the most delicious toast you've ever had in your life, Linda?!" said Dad. We all gathered around the oven.

"Can I wash my hands first?" said Mom, "or is the flavor peaking this very *second*."

"Linda, this is no time for sarcasm. Just wash your hands and sit down and relax," said Dad, "and I'll serve you! You too, kids."

Mom washed her hands at the sink, and Lucy, Danny, and I sat down at the table.

"I poured the juice," said Danny.

"You did a great job," Mom smiled as she joined us. "No spills."

"O-kee do-kee!" sang Dad as he opened the oven and brought out the plates. "Hot plates for everybody! Dad's special method!"

He set one in front of each of us.

"Thanks, honey," Mom said.

"Thanks, Dad!!" we all chimed. It did feel like a special occasion. A party, almost, the way he did it.

"And now . . . the *pièce de résistance*! My crowning achievement! The main event! Ladies and gentlemen . . . DAD'S SPECIAL TOAST!!!"

He set the big plate of warm, crispy, buttery cinnamon toast in the center of the table.

"YAAAAAAAY!" we all cheered. "Hooray for Daaaaaad!" we applauded.

Dad took a bow and sat down to eat.

Everybody took a couple of pieces of toast and starting oohing and aahing like mad.

"*UNBELIEVABLE!*" said Lucy. "The best I've ever had! By far!"

"FRIGHTENINGLY good," said Mom. "Beyond toast. Indescribably delicious."

"Extraterrestrial," I said. "Yummy in the tummy."

We all munched in silence for a minute.

Then Danny spoke up.

"What's the big deal?" said Danny. "All he did was make toast."

"Danny!" Lucy scolded. "That's not very nice! It's really *great* toast!"

"*Perfect* toast!" I cried.

"*Warm* toast!" Mom added.

We all went back to munching.

"But Mom does a million times more housework every *day*, and we hardly even thank her at all! And we *never* go 'Yaaaay.' "

We all looked at Danny.

Then we all looked at Mom.

on the *following* day. My schoolmates were all giggles, but I felt totally humiliated. Luckily, my mother hadn't left the bus stop. I got off the bus and ran into her arms.

With tears streaming down my cheeks, I begged her to let me go home and change. But she wouldn't. Since she didn't drive, there was no way for me to get to school. And she refused to let me stay home. I've never forgiven my mother for that incident, nor forgotten that awful day. More than two decades later, the hurt still haunts me. I suspect it always will.

Perhaps that painful memory is the reason I become panic-stricken when I have to dress up for a party, a wedding, or an interview. I rummage through my closet and drawers, scared about making the wrong decision. When I finally settle on an outfit, I dress with dread, convinced I'll walk into a room looking totally out of place.

For me, the memory of that ill-fated costume is as vivid as any photograph in our family album. But recently, when I mentioned it to my mother, she completely denied that the incident had occurred. "In fact," she insisted, "I remember coming on the bus with you to look at the other kids' getups."

One of us is rewriting my biography. Mom may be right. Perhaps my version is simply a recreation of what might have happened. Or, my mother may have recast the event because she can't accept the decision she made that morning twenty-five years ago. There's no way to be sure. Yet the incident is deeply ingrained in my memory, and the feelings that remain are powerful.

Lee Kaufman, a restaurant manager I know, also has uncomfortable memories that affect her even today. Once a pudgy child, Lee is always afraid that if she doesn't exercise every day, she'll blossom overnight into the chubby little girl in her old pictures. "I was a bundle of baby fat long after I stopped toddling," Lee says. "In fact, I can still hear the 'foosh foosh' of my corduroy pants as my thighs rubbed together when I walked home from school.

"My worst moment was at my friend Sandy's birthday party. I was wearing my favorite dress with big puff sleeves and a very short, flared skirt. It wasn't particularly becoming for a little butterball, but I felt like a princess whenever I wore it. But *all* that changed when I overheard Sandy's mother talking about me to some of the other mothers sitting on the couch. As I was being spun around to pin the tail on the donkey, I heard her say, 'How can Lee's mother let her daughter wear a dress like that, with those *enormous* fleshy thighs?' I can still feel my face burning red with embarrassment. I felt big and ugly. A little voice inside me vowed I would never grow up fat. I still hear that voice whenever I'm tempted to give in to the munchies or give up on my exercises.''

It's not a childhood voice that influences Erin Tadd, a college senior, years later, but a frightening memory of her stern third-grade teacher. "One day Mrs. Bennet announced she was going to audition everyone in our class for the glee club,'' says Erin. "Those who could sing would be excused from class one hour a week for practice, but those who had a 'tin ear' would not.

"When my turn came around, I was hopeless from the start. My voice cracked, my notes went sour, and I sang so quietly that Mrs. Bennet screamed, 'Louder! Louder!' I wanted to fall through the floor. In the end, the worst thing that could have happened happened: I was *the only one in the class* who didn't make the glee club. But it taught me to be strong during those dejected Thursday afternoons when everyone else was at choral practice.''

Erin hasn't gotten over her fear of singing in front of people. Even joining in a round of "Happy Birthday" has her frozen solid, silently mouthing the words. "If I'm ever asked to sing, I always say, 'I can't. I'm tone deaf.' No amount of prodding will get me to put myself on the line again.''

Not all memories are so threatening; some are fond recollections that influence us in positive ways. Beth Jarvis, a New York copywriter, vividly recalls an autumn afternoon spent with her father in Minnesota, where she grew up. "We walked along the railroad tracks and my father spoke about how he had met my mother and about their love and commitment. Then he picked up a stone, and turned it around in his hand. 'When you love someone,' he said, 'it's a responsibility. Not something you can throw away . . . like this stone.' As he flung the stone along the railroad tracks, I watched it hopscotch in the distance.

"My father's talk made a lasting impression on me," Beth says. "I've grown to approach relationships with a certain reverence. Maybe that's why, though my friends weave in and out of relationships, I've stayed with my boyfriend for five years, and we're stronger than ever.''

Memories not only light up moments in our past, but illuminate present emotions as well. Recently, I recalled an afternoon when my mother and I sat at our kitchen table, working on a diorama based on a book I had read. Mom gave me ideas and helped cut and paste the little house constructed inside the shoe box. As I recalled her attention and support, I felt incredibly grateful and I wanted to thank her for all she had done for me. So that evening, I wrote her a note.

Memories such as these have helped nourish my life. Memories are the landscapes in our minds where the people and events we'll never forget, for better or worse, live forever. We all have them. So what are your special memories?

RESPONSE

1. Assuming the incident happened as the author remembers it, what do you think of the mother's decision to send the costumed child on to school in the school bus?
2. Explain what the author means when she writes, "memories not only light up . . . our past, but illuminate present emotions as well."

EXTENSION

3. "Memories are the landscapes in our minds where the people and events we'll never forget, for better or worse, live forever." Illustrate the truth of this statement with a memory from your own life.
4. In your journal, write about an event from your childhood in which your behaviour caused embarrassment for your parents.

INSTEAD OF *SAFE* SEX, WHY NOT *SAVE* SEX?

MARIE G. LEE

- Write a dialogue which could take place between a boy and a girl.
- Review all of the dialogues written by the class and perform some of them.
- What conclusions can you draw from these dialogues?

One night last year, I ignored all my studying to accompany some friends to a small lecture hall at Brown University where Dr. Ruth (Westheimer, the well-known therapist who dispenses advice about sexual problems on radio and TV) was to make a guest appearance.

She was certainly funny and had a charming accent, but although I agreed with her themes, I disagreed with her approach. She had a lot to say about the way young people make love and offered plenty of tips and new ideas. She also stressed "safe" sex via condoms: Men should keep them in their wallets; women should start carrying their own (for protection, and, Dr. Ruth pointed out, "because they now come in colors to coordinate with every outfit").

In praising all the virtues of "safe" sex and "fun" sex and "good" sex, not once did Dr. Ruth mention "saved" sex. With all the discussion concerning frequency of sex, kinds of sex, and numbers of sexual partners, the listener came away with the feeling that it was normal — indeed healthy — to be engaging regularly in lusty and gymnastic bouts of sex. Love didn't seem to enter into the matter. Dr. Ruth had a lot of ideas for making good sex better, but she never seemed to consider that sometimes the "better" sexual choice is not to have sex.

I have many friends who admit they wish they had not started having sexual relations in their teens — they claim it tended to dull their enjoyment later on. I was lucky enough to have made the "why-don't-I-wait-a-little-longer" decision, which turns out to have given me much more long-term satisfaction, I think, than I would have gotten by deciding to become sexually active much earlier. In high school, I somehow got the notion that those four years were the last ones of my youth, and I ought to live it up. I had boyfriends, and several times I thought very seriously about having sex. After all, I was in love (or so I thought) each time; and, after freshman year, most of my friends were having sex.

By my junior year I had been dating my boyfriend, a senior, for about a year. He decided it was time to "cement" our relationship. He was very tender about it, offering to be responsible for protecting us, and promising that this would be very, very special. I was teetering right on the edge, but in the end I stalled. My boyfriend became testy; still, I jumped to the safety of abstinence. When we broke up soon after, I thought I would be crying for the rest of my life. Now looking back, it seems to have been quite a bit less than a life-or-death matter, and I can see that I did not want to sleep with him except to appease him.

College was the next step, and if anything, it served to prove that life did extend beyond high school. It also raised a lot more questions about my sexual attitudes. At Brown it certainly seemed as if everyone were sleeping with everyone else. At night, listening to the slamming dorm room doors, I'd think, "I saved myself for this?"

But my concerns soon extended beyond merely the sexual arena. I began to realize that I had the resources, and the freedom, to make myself into the person I wanted to be. What I observed of girls who slept around did not seem very appealing. They didn't appear to be any happier, savvier, or more concerned with life than girls who were not sexually "sophisticated." In fact, some seemed even more hyper — contrary to the myth that "good" sex brings true serenity. I began to feel quite comfortable spending my nights with a typewriter or book. I still had frequent fears of missing out on fun, or worse, maybe I'd never have another boyfriend! But the feelings didn't last, especially after I learned to trust my instincts first.

I graduated from college *sans sexe* — maybe they should have printed that on my diploma; it was quite an accomplishment — and moved to New York. For the year that I've lived here, I've been surprised by how many of my newly graduated women friends assume that dating and sex go hand in hand. Funny thing: A lot of my male friends have expressed the opinion that life would be a lot simpler if they could have a good time with a young woman on the first date without worrying whether she is expecting a *good time.*

For me, the lack of personal sexual history is just one facet of my personality, but one that works with the whole individual. Although I am not saving sex for any one special time or for one special person, it gives me satisfaction to know I have not become sexually involved for any of the "wrong" reasons: because all my friends are doing it; because Dr. Ruth says it's healthy to do it; because ads/songs/TV shows tell us the beautiful people are beautiful because they can get regular sex.

For now, I am seriously partnered with a "hunk"; a former classmate at Brown who also managed to get through high school and college without doing "it." How about that. He likes to read and write, too.

1. What are the conflicting messages which our society sends to young people about sex?

2. "... it gives me satisfaction to know I have not become sexually involved for any of the 'wrong' reasons ..." According to Lee, what are the "wrong" reasons? Do you agree?

USING LANGUAGE

DON'T TALK DIRTY TO ME

RUSSELL BAKER

- Does "dirty talk" ever make you feel uncomfortable? Explain.
- Do you think it is ever appropriate to use "dirty talk"? Explain.

There was another one of those smoke fights on an airplane the other day. It's always the same: a smoker so desperate for a cigarette he's ready to start screaming in pain. Somebody willing to die rather than be subjected to cigarette smoke. Pandemonium in the sky, police meeting the plane at the gate. Much assertion of human rights vis à vis tobacco smoke.

Having tried both ways of life, tobacco-stained and nicotine-free, I sympathize with both sides, but pray I never end up on one of those planes where they fight it out. I use the words "end up" by design. It's bad enough up there when you're wondering whether the pilot is using something to revise his brain. We don't need passenger riots to put the thrill back into air travel.

Still, the passion of the smoke haters is phenomenal. You don't see comparable fury applied to curbing any other social habit, like, say, getting drunk or talking dirty.

This last is a particular grievance of mine. Sidestream smoke, as the Surgeon General reports, may rot lungs, heart and other innards, but dirty talk rots the mind, and I'd like to see a vigorous, aggressive campaign waged against the people who do it. When you try to get a clean talk movement started, though, people think you're joking.

At the airport, for instance: "Smoking or nonsmoking?" they ask. What do I care? I have smoked and I have non-smoked, and can put up with either condition.

What I'd rather be asked is, "Dirty talking or non-dirty talking?" I have dirty talked and I have non-dirty talked, and I never want to dirty talk again or associate with the kind of people who do. For two years in the military I lived immersed in dirty talk. If Eddie Murphy had come into our outfit and started talking, we would have washed out his mouth with mud for talking clean.

Near the end of my tour, a trusted companion asked, "Hey, you (dirty talk)ing (dirty talk)er. What the (dirty talk) you gonna do when those (dirty talk)ing (dirty talk)s hand you the (dirty talk), (dirty talk), (dirty talk) pen and ask you to (dirty talk)ing sign up for another two (dirty talk)ing years?"

"I'm (dirty talk)ing gonna tell the (dirty talk)ing, (dirty talk)s to take that (dirty talk)ing pen and shove it . . ."

At this point I broke down and told my friend, "I'm getting out, pal."

"You're (dirty talk)ing kidding!" he expostulated.

"I mean it," I said. "I want to go once again to a place where a man can ask, 'What in the world do you think you're doing?' and 'Isn't this a devil of a mess?' and 'By George, he's got it; I think he's got it!' without being exiled for talking weird."

I am not an absolutist on this. Live and let live is my philosophy. Jonathan Yardley of *The Washington Post* recently noted the spread of vile language into almost every movie made for adolescents, which is almost every movie made nowadays. This suggests that American youth is now as firmly hooked on dirty talk as its parents once were on nicotine.

Just as millions of those parents have broken their cigarette addiction, so millions of American youngsters can probably break their dependence on dirty talk. It would be cruel, however, to expect them to break the habit cold turkey. Few of their parents were able to give up cigarettes without a struggle; few of the children find it easy to free themselves from their enslavement to vile and foul-mouthed speech.

For humane reasons, then, an all-out attack on dirty talk would be excessively cruel. We must proceed gradually, subtly. Just inside doorways, windows or attic dormers . . . let us place small signs that say, "Thank you for not talking dirty."

Let taxicab drivers plaster the interiors of their cars with stickers that say, "No vile language. Driver allergic to dirty talk."

Let restaurants establish dirty talking sections for diners too weak to break the chains that bind them.

A ban on dirty talk in movies and television? Absolutely not! No censorship! Never!

With sufficient bullying by an aroused public, however, theatre marquees and printed television schedules might carry the message: "Warning: This entertainment contains dirty talk which may . . . create the depressing illusion that you are trapped in a military barracks with people who think you are weird."

Crusaders against smoke want everybody to live longer, but if it means everybody will have more years to spend talking dirty, what's the point?

RESPONSE

1. Do you agree with Baker that adolescents are "hooked on dirty talk"?
2. What do you think of Baker's suggestion that society ban "dirty talk" in public places?

EXTENSION

3. In your journal, examine your own attitude towards "dirty talk." For example, do you ever use "dirty talk"? When? What do you think of people who "talk dirty"? Do you feel strange among your friends if you don't "talk dirty"?
4. In your group, devise a set of rules for language use which your class will follow. You might like to consider eliminating language which is sexist, racist, or abusive in some other way.

HOW TO WRITE A LETTER

GARRISON KEILLOR

- Discuss with your group the last time you wrote or received a personal letter.
- List some of the things which could be written in a letter that could not be said in a telephone conversation.

W e shy persons need to write a letter now and then, or else we'll dry up and blow away. It's true. And I speak as one who loves to reach for the phone, dial the number, and talk. I say, "Big Bopper here — what's shakin', babes?" The telephone is to shyness what Hawaii is to February, it's a way out of the woods, *and yet*: a letter is better.

Such a sweet gift — a piece of handmade writing, in an envelope that is not a bill, sitting in our friend's path when she trudges home from a long day spent among wahoos and savages, a day our words will help repair. They don't need to be immortal, just sincere. She can read them twice and again tomorrow: *You're someone I care about, Corinne, and think of often and every time I do you make me smile.*

We need to write, otherwise nobody will know who we are. They will have only a vague impression of us as A Nice Person, because, frankly, we don't shine at conversation, we lack the confidence to thrust our faces forward and say, "Hi, I'm Heather Hooten; let me tell you about my week." Mostly we say "Uh-huh" and "Oh, really." People smile and look over our shoulder, looking for someone else to meet.

So a shy person sits down and writes a letter. To be known by another person — to meet and talk freely on the page — to be close despite distance. To escape from anonymity and be our own sweet selves and express the music of our souls.

Same thing that moves a giant rock star to sing his heart out in front of 123 000 people moves us to take ballpoint in hand and write a few lines to our dear Aunt Eleanor. *We want to be known.* We want her to know that we have fallen in love, that we quit our job, that we're moving to New York, and we want to say a few things that might not get said in casual conversation: *Thank you for what you've meant to me, I am very happy right now.*

The first step in writing letters is to get over the guilt of *not* writing. You don't "owe" anybody a letter. Letters are a gift. The burning shame you feel when you see unanswered mail makes it harder to pick up a pen and makes for a cheerless letter when you finally do. *I feel bad about not writing, but I've been so busy,* etc. Skip this. Few letters are obligatory, and they are *Thanks for the wonderful gift* and *I am terribly sorry to hear about George's death* and *Yes, you're welcome to stay with us next month,* and not many more than that. Write those promptly if you want to keep your friends. Don't worry about the others, except love letters, of course. When your true love writes, *Dear Light of My Life, Joy of My Heart, O Lovely Pulsating Core of My Sensate Life,* some response is called for.

Some of the best letters are tossed off in a burst of inspiration, so keep your writing stuff in one place where you can sit down for a few minutes and (*Dear Roy, I am in the middle of a book entitled* We Are Still Married *but I thought I'd drop you a line. Hi to your sweetie, too*) dash off a note to a pal. Envelopes, stamps, address book, everything in a drawer so you can write fast when the pen is hot.

A blank white eight-by-eleven sheet can look as big as Montana if the pen's not so hot — try a smaller page and write boldly. Or use a note card with a piece of fine art on the front; if your letter ain't good, at least they get the Matisse. Get a pen that makes a sensuous line, get a comfortable typewriter, a friendly word processor — whichever feels easy to the hand.

Sit for a few minutes with the blank sheet in front of you, and meditate on the person you will write to, let your friend come to mind until you can almost see her or him in the room with you. Remember the last time you saw each other and how your friend looked and what you said and what perhaps was unsaid between you, and when your friend becomes real to you, start to write.

Write the salutation — *Dear* You — and take a deep breath and plunge in. A simple declarative sentence will do, followed by another and another and another. Tell us what you're doing and tell it like you were talking to us. Don't think about grammar, don't think about lit'ry style, don't try to write dramatically, just give us your news. Where did you go, who did you see, what did they say, what do you think?

If you don't know where to begin, start with the present moment: *I'm sitting at the kitchen table on a rainy Saturday morning. Everyone is gone and the house is quiet.* Let your simple description of the present moment lead to something else, let the letter drift gently along.

The toughest letter to crank out is one that is meant to impress, as we all know from writing job applications; if it's hard work to slip off a letter to a friend, maybe you're trying too hard to be terrific. A letter is only a report to someone who already likes you for reasons other than your brilliance. Take it easy.

Don't worry about form. It's not a term paper. When you come to the end of one episode, just start a new paragraph. You can go from a few lines about the sad state of pro football to the fight with your mother to your fond memories of Mexico to your cat's urinary-tract infection to a few thoughts on personal indebtedness and on to the kitchen sink and what's in it. The more you write, the easier it gets, and when you have a True True Friend to write to, a *compadre*, a soul sibling, then it's like driving a car down a country road, you just get behind the keyboard and press on the gas.

Don't tear up the page and start over when you write a bad line — try to write your way out of it. Make mistakes and plunge on. Let the letter cook along and let yourself be bold. Outrage, confusion, love — whatever is in your mind, let it find a way to the page. Writing is a means of discovery, always, and when you come to the end and write *Yours ever* or *Hugs and kisses*, you'll know something you didn't when you wrote *Dear Pal.*

Probably your friend will put your letter away, and it'll be read again a few years from now — and it will improve with age. And forty years from now, your friend's grandkids will dig it out of the attic and read it, a sweet and precious relic of the ancient eighties that gives them a sudden clear glimpse of you and her and the world we old-timers knew. You will then have created an object of art. Your simple lines about where you went, who you saw, what they said, will speak to those children and they will feel in their hearts the humanity of our times.

You can't pick up a phone and call the future and tell them about our times. You have to pick up a piece of paper.

RESPONSE

1. What do you think the author means when he writes the following lines?
   a) "We need to write, otherwise nobody will know who we are."
   b) "Writing is a means of discovery, always . . . ."
   c) ". . . to meet and talk freely on the page — to be close despite distance."
   d) "You can't pick up a phone and call the future and tell them about our times. You have to pick up a piece of paper."

EXTENSION

2. Bring to class an old letter which you have received or which a family member has received. Discuss with your group what you can learn from the letter about the person who wrote it.
3. Write a letter to yourself. You may wish to address yourself in the third person. Use some of Keillor's advice as to what to write about and how to write it. Seal the letter in an envelope and have your teacher keep all the letters until the last day of classes.
4. Write and mail a letter to a person who means a great deal to you. Start the letter right now!

PEOPLE AND THEIR MACHINES AND VICE VERSA

PETER GZOWSKI

- Explain how the word processor has changed the way you write.
- Would you ever consider a career as a professional writer or journalist? Explain.

f I have remembered my own history correctly, it is exactly thirty years ago this week that I arrived in Timmins, Ontario, to begin my life as a newspaperman. Almost every day for those thirty years, I have opened my working procedures the same way. I have cranked a piece of paper into my typewriter, banged out what newspapermen call a slug at the top of the page, usually followed, for reasons I don't know but by a habit I can't break, by the page number typed four or five times, and started pounding away with as many fingers as seemed to fit. Like most old newspapermen, I am as fast as a Gatling gun at my machine, and almost as noisy. I make mistakes — which is like saying Wayne Gretzky gets scoring points — but I strike them out: xxxxxxx or, if I'm really flying, mnmnmnmnmnmn, *m* with the right forefinger, *n* with the left. Afterward, I go over what I've done with the heaviest pencil I can find, changing a word here, a phrase there. I cross out some more, with a bold, black stroke and a flourishing delete sign. I add. Sometimes I make what one of my editors called chicken tracks from the place I had the first thought out into the margin. Out there, I create anew. I scribble up into the bare space at the top, up by the stammering page numbers, and on good days, when my juices are flowing and the ghost of Maxwell Perkins is looking over my shoulder, I carry on from there, turning the page under my pencil, down the outer edges, filling the bottom and off, off into virgin territories, leaving my inky spoor behind me. When I am pleased with what I have done, or when the chicken tracks get too dense to follow, I put a new page in the typewriter and start again. This is not the way anyone taught me to work. But it is the way I have done things. It has served me through five books, more magazine articles than you could shake an art director's ruler at and enough newspaper pieces to line the cage of every eagle that ever flew.

But no more. I am a word-processor man now, or trying to become one. I made the change at the end of this summer. The words I am reading to you now first appeared to my eye etched in green on a dark screen. Or, rather, some *version* of the words I am reading to you now so appeared. "Green," for instance, was "gereen," or perhaps "jereen," until I danced my cursor around the screen (the "scereen?") and obliterated the extra *e*. "Etched," too, is probably the wrong word. The process by which these words appear is too sophisticated for my manually operated mind, and I no more understand it than I understand what really happens when I turn on the ignition of my car. All I know, in fact, are two things: one, I can do it. If I take my time, and think my way through such delicate differences as that between the "control" key and the shift lock, and resist the urge to hit the space bar (which makes sense to me) and instead hit a simultaneous "control" and *d* (which doesn't) when I want to move my little cursor over one notch, I can, however painstakingly, make the words come out in prose. That's one. Two is that I hate doing it. Over the years, the relationship I have built up with my various manuals is an emotional one. I pound them and they respond, as the Steinway responded to Glenn Gould. I knew I was working because I could hear it, and the measure of what I had accomplished in a working day was often the pile of out-takes that grew in my wastepaper basket, like tailings at a mine. Now, I work silently. I wrote what you are hearing now while my daughter slept in the next room. This was convenient for Alison, but it did not seem to me to be what I have always done for a living. It neither sounded nor felt like *writing*. God, it seems to me, no more meant words to appear in fluorescent electronic letters than he meant pool tables to be pink, or golf balls orange.

RESPONSE

1. Are there any similarities between the writing process you use and the one that Peter Gzowski uses? Explain.
2. What do you think about Gzowski's attitude toward his typewriter and his word processor?

EXTENSION

3. a) Research the invention of the typewriter and the QWERTY keyboard.
   b) Why did the manufacturers of personal computers retain the QWERTY keyboard?
4. Write a short composition about a machine that is important to you.

THE DIRTY DOZEN

WAYNE GRADY

- In groups, invent a unit of measurement to measure both the area and volume of your classroom without reference to either the metric or the imperial systems of measurement.
- Convince the other groups that your unit of measurement should be adopted universally.

Dear Sir,

W*hy, oh why, does Harrowsmith persist in pretending that we are still in the Dark Ages? You may not realize it, but the rest of the civilized world has long since gone metric. Our children learn only the metric system in school, and we all must go through considerable mental gymnastics in order to make sense of your gardening and construction articles. Harrowsmith is a modern magazine, even an avant-garde one in many ways, so why not bring it into the twentieth century in this respect too?*

Yours truly,
A Metre Reader

Dear A. Reader,

I like to play chess. I started playing chess when I was 12 years old. That year, my best friend received a red-and-black plastic Staunton Design chess set for Christmas, and he and I sat down at the kitchen table and puzzled out the "Basic Moves and Strategies" sheet that came with it. The most popular opening move, according to the sheet, was to move the Pawn in front of the King two squares forward to the fourth square. This move apparently established control of the centre squares, opened up developing lanes for the Queen and King's Bishop and provided an escape hatch for the Queen's Knight. The move was called "Pawn to King Four" — in chess notation, written P-K4.

I developed an affection for P-K4. In later years, I learned that P-K4 is the first move of the Ruy López opening, but never mind that. What I liked about P-K4 was that I could look at it and know what it meant. It meant Pawn to King Four. When Bobby Fischer played Boris Spassky in Reykjavik for the World Chess Championship and the newspapers reported that Bobby's opening move in game three was P-K4, I could picture him picking up the King's Pawn with his long, violinist's fingers and setting it down on square four. There was something warm about P-K4. It depicted movement, it represented something visual, something alive.

These days, P-K4 is written e4. At some point, a committee in charge of chess notation decided that P-K4 was too cumbersome, or too ambiguous, or too long, or too old, and changed it to e4. I do not like e4. I cannot look at e4 and see movement, or warmth, or a human hand picking up a chess piece and setting it down again on a square. What I see is a computer programme, a digital readout. I see words like "matrix" and "praxis" — e4 is not a move, it is a point on a grid.

A very similar thing has happened with weights and measures, it seems to me. What I liked about P-K4 was that I could look at it and see words: Pawn, King. And those words connected in my imagination with real flesh-and-blood beings, to a time when kings fought on battlefields, leading armies of pawns and knights against enemy-held castles. The old chess notations used words that had grown out of history and culture. So do some of the old Imperial units of measurement. The Troy pound, for instance, which is still used by goldsmiths and apothecaries, was named in the twelfth century after the city of Troyes, in France, because the merchants there could be trusted to give good measure. I feel no such historical reverberations when I seen the word "gram."

Historically, of course, both systems have merit. The Romans liked the number 10. Their army was divided into legions consisting of 3,000 soldiers, commanded by centurions, quinquagenarians and decans. The history of their empire was arranged into decades and centuries. Their year consisted of 10 months, the seventh, eighth, ninth and tenth of which were called September, October, November and December. They decimated their enemies — that is, they lined up their prisoners and killed every tenth one. Many of those prisoners were people who had their own measuring systems, based not on some abstract, arbitrarily chosen division but on things they could see and touch, on parts of their own bodies or on the size of their own land. A yard (from an Old English word meaning "stick") was the length of a rag merchant's arm, an inch (from the Latin word for "one-twelfth") was the width of a carpenter's thumb, and a furlong (short for "furrow-long") was the length of a farmer's field.

After the Roman conquest, the Roman system of measurement, like the Latin language, began to turn up in odd ways and in odd places. For example, the Romans divided longer distances into marching units of 1,000 paces (*milia passum*), which corresponded to roughly 5,000 feet. The English rounded that off to 8 furlongs (5,280 feet) but kept the Latin name for it: mile. However, they kept most of their own soil-based units intact. The barleycorn, for instance, was used to measure smallness: 3 barleycorns equal 1 inch. We still use the barleycorn today, even in these metric times; the difference in length between a size 7 shoe and a size 8 shoe is 1 barleycorn.

Proponents of the metric system say it is more scientific because everything in it is based on the number 10. I say there is nothing intrinsically superior about a system based on 10 over a system based on 12. In fact, mathematically, 12 is a better number than 10, since 12 can be divided by 2, 3, 4 and 6, whereas 10 can be divided only by 2 and 5. I also like the look of the word "twelve" better than "ten," but that's got nothing to do with science. So 12 works very nicely and, unlike 10, slides easily into every system of measurement we have. There are 12 inches in a foot, 12 Troy ounces in a Troy pound, 12 dozen in a gross, 24 hours in a day, 12 months in a year and 360 degrees in a circle. During the French Revolution, there was an attempt to reform the solar calendar by dividing the year into 12 months of 30 days each, each 10-day "week" to be called a decade. But no one could figure out what to do with the other 5 days, so the project was dropped. And no one has ever, ever been able to metricate the circle. You cannot slice a pi.

The Age of Reason did succeed in changing the yard to the metre, however, and what a marvellous joke that has been. The idea was to base the kilometre on a measurement of the Earth's surface (as if the mile were not). An imaginary line was drawn from the Earth's equator to the North Pole, passing through Paris. This line, called a quadrant, was divided into 10 million units, each of which was called a metre (from the Latin *metrum*, or measure). Unfortunately, since no one had ever been to the North Pole and since the instrument they used to compute the curvature of the Earth's surface had been dropped in the ocean and got all rusty, they miscalculated the length of the quadrant: instead of 10 million metres, it turned out to be 10,002,228.3 metres. But they had already sold a lot of metre-sticks, so they just kept quiet about it; besides, if they recalculated the metre using the new measurement, it would have ended up being almost exactly the same length as a yard, and they couldn't have that. It all took place long ago, anyway, in another century. Now we have a new definition of "metre," based on purely scientifically verifiable and repeatable observations. The metre is equal to 1,553,164.13 wavelengths of red light emitted from a heated sample of the metal cadmium. Now, isn't that handy?

If learning the Imperial system is like learning a second language, there is nothing wrong with learning a second language. And if I were an educator instead of a magazine editor, I wouldn't mind putting people through some mental gymnastics.

RESPONSE

1. In your groups, review the origins of the units of measurement presented by the author. In your opinion, which one makes the most sense?

EXTENSION

2. Explain why there are 24 hours in a day. Why are there 360 degrees in a circle? Why do we still sell eggs by the dozen?
3. Explain in detail one of the historical references made by the author (e.g., the organization of the Roman army). Report your findings to your group.

DON'T WAIT FOR THE MOVIE

GORDON KORMAN

- Develop a questionnaire to survey the reading habits of your class.
- What conclusions can you draw from the results of your survey?

I remember a conversation with a producer who was working on turning one of my books into a feature film. The more I heard, the more I became convinced that I had better savour the moment when "Based on the Novel by . . ." flashed on the screen, because it was going to be the only thing in the movie even vaguely reminiscent of what I wrote.

I think it finally sank in when the producer said, "Well, you know the scene where Steve — ?"

"Wait a second," I interrupted. "Who's Steve?"

How ignorant of me to think that, as the guy who wrote the book, I should actually be able to recognize the hero, especially after they plotted, replotted, unplotted, added, excised, and replaced personnel like Harold Ballard. Can't tell the players without a scorecard.

Then I thought of the junior high school student who might someday be called upon to do a book report on my book. He would plow over to the video store to rent *that* movie, save time, and come up with a report destined to flunk with flying colours. (The character sketch of Steve would lay a particularly large egg.) Every one of us has beaten a deadline by condensing a lot of reading time into a 90-minute movie.

All this is hypothetical, of course, because the proposed movie never got made — which is why I am not dictating this piece over the cellular phone in my Maserati. But it did get me thinking about book versus movie, and what makes a book so special, since it obviously isn't time efficiency.

Lately, teachers have thrown us a curve. Now we have to read the book *and* see the movie, and compare the two. Teachers are very big on comparisons. Here it works. Almost invariably, the book gets the nod.

That's not to say that all the movies are bad. After the books, though, they're just somehow incomplete. The novel always seems to have something more — a greater depth, a different perspective, a more incisive insight and humour. There is something unique to the written word — to that relationship between author and reader — which cannot be reproduced any other way. It's more than just reporting or storytelling. It's *different*.

A reader participates in a novel. In a sense, it is almost a collaboration between him and the writer as, reading, he supplies his own interpretation — the reader's draft. No two are ever alike. You can read the same book as someone else without reading the same book. (For instance, everybody who read *Lord Jim* and liked it read a different book than I did. That may be because I'm a poor "collaborator" with Joseph Conrad.) There is a feeling of accomplishment when you come to the end of a very good book — you have completed a successful collaboration. Don't expect royalties.

This is all coming from someone who was a staunch non-reader in elementary school. Once, in a book report, just to avoid actually reading anything, I went so far as to make up an entire novel, characters and all, using my friend's kid sister as the writer. There was even a section on "other books by the same author," and an excerpt from the *Boston Globe* review. It took ten times as much energy as doing the assignment properly, but to me, no amount of figuring the angles was unjustified. I didn't want to read, period. I got an A. Crime pays.

What finally hooked me in was humour. When I found books that made me laugh, my sense of the "work" of reading was replaced by something wonderful and totally unfamiliar — a desire to find what happened next. It was a crucial connection. From then on, I equated reading with enjoying myself, and I was a reader for good.

This may sound like an oversimplification, but beware. Relating reading and enjoyment can't be taught; it has to happen. It's a click. Without that click, no amount of explanation, no pleading, no assurance that this is a "great story," will do any good. In my case, humour produced the desired click. But mystery, suspense, adventure, science-fiction, romance, and nonfiction can do the job too. I tend to stick with the funny stuff as the best bet. Tastes can be very specialized, but just about everybody loves to laugh.

My father used to summarize his reading history with the statement, "I read a book once," which was, unfortunately, not greatly exaggerated. Then, out of parental loyalty, he started reading my work. But when I didn't seem to be churning them out fast enough, he tried other authors, and found that you don't have to be a blood relative to appreciate good writing. Now it's not uncommon to find him with a good book in his hand. Reading helps you develop a facility for language, which in turn helps you to read. A neat circle.

Being literate, by definition, is being able to read and write and function in society with these acquired skills. After that, you're on your own, and your reading is what you yourself choose to make of it. Education and reading material are abundant in Canada, and sharing with the rest of the world is something we are fortunate to be able to do. But we, who have all the advantages, often lack something the disadvantaged have to a man — motivation. Too many of our kids don't *want* to read. They equate reading exclusively with work and school — something that is done only under duress, never voluntarily. I had one childhood friend whose parents actually used it as punishment; the greater the infraction, the more days he would have to spend reading. I've lost touch with him, but I'm pretty sure he reads nothing to this day. Would you?

We have to play up the entertainment side of reading as our kids take their first step towards books. If they latch onto a topic that grabs them, the books will do the rest. Then, in the all-important war for rapidly dwindling leisure time, reading will have a fighting chance with the big boys — hockey, MuchMusic, *Friday the 13th: Part 173*, and Super Mega-Deluxe Mario Brothers 40. We don't have to wipe out the competition (we haven't got a prayer, and we shouldn't want to) but it would be nice to be on the program.

I once got a letter from a ten-year-old boy who wrote: "I hate reading, but your books are different. I'm going to read them all." It was not only flattering and good business, but also encouraging. I *know* that kid will discover, as he develops the reading habit with my stuff, a lot of other authors who are "different," and that he'll go on to be a real reader.

Chalk one up for our side.

RESPONSE

1. In your groups, discuss which of the following statements you agree with.
   a) "After books, [movies are] just somehow incomplete."
   b) "Relating reading and enjoyment can't be taught [and] no amount of explanation . . . will do any good."
   c) "Too many of our kids don't want to read."

EXTENSION

2. Read one of Korman's books. Write a letter to him, care of his publisher, and let him know what you thought of the book.
3. Arrange with your teacher for your group to read a novel and view a video based on that novel. Compare the two.

EXCEPTIONAL LIVES

INTERVIEW WITH ROBERTA BONDAR

HOWARD A. DOUGHTY

- What sort of education do you think a person needs to become an astronaut?
- Do you think that all students acquire the same quality of education in high school? Explain.

R oberta Bondar is one of the six Canadian astronauts selected for Canada's Space Program. Chairperson of the Lifesciences Subcommittee for Space Station, she is one of those being considered as a payload specialist in a future shuttle mission. Her credentials include a B.Sc. in zoology and agriculture from the University of Guelph, an M.Sc. in experimental pathology from the University of Western Ontario, a Ph.D. in neurobiology from the University of Toronto and an M.D. from McMaster University in Hamilton.

Doughty: What, in your early life, guided you toward a career in science?

Bondar: My parents are not from a science background. They came through high school during the depression, so neither of them was able to go on to university. But they were interested in biology and often took the family tenting when we were really young. They were always interested in the things we did, so we never felt like kids in an adult world. We were all there together existing on this planet and learning about things. It didn't matter what project we had; it never seemed too small. They never pushed us in any one direction. My sister was interested in the arts, and I liked sports and science, but they were always right there to encourage us.

Doughty: *What about other influences?*

Bondar: When I was in grade seven, I think, I had a science teacher who was interested in showing us how experiments worked. I was really turned on by the whole business. My dad had some chemistry equipment from when he was in high school and I got some stuff from my uncle, who was a pharmacist. Then, I went to my grandmother's basement and my dad helped me build a little laboratory there. Later, in high school, I got involved in one of the very early science fairs. I did a project on the forest tent caterpillar because I was really influenced by Rachel Carson's book, *Silent Spring*.

Doughty: *And then you went on to university?*

Bondar: Yes. I was very torn between physical education and science. My ideal was to be a high school gym and science teacher, but in those days you couldn't get a combined honours degree in those subjects. I started going for a B.Sc., hoping to get a B.P.H.E. later, but because of some health problems and some injuries, I decided to just go on in science.

Doughty: *Were there any special events along the way?*

Bondar: In those days there were prizes for the best boy and the best girl in high school science fairs. So, I got to go to the Canada-wide Science Fair and met a lot of other young men and women who were also doing projects, and I also managed to get a job at the local forest insect laboratory, where one of the chaps helped me on my project. I worked there for the next six summers. That was really important because I was able to see what kinds of things science *did* without reading about it in books.

Doughty: *How do you think your success can both act as a role model for students and for society's leaders?*

Bondar: The problem with our country, I think, is that we have a national mandate for science and provincial mandates for education. That's a real difficulty. Now, I'm not a social science teacher, so I'm just telling you gut stuff here, but in order to change we have to identify what we want to change. We need people who are creative and who are not afraid of science. Students have problems with peer pressure and parental attitudes. It doesn't matter much if the schools have a good science program, if, at the same time, young people are being told one thing by one group and another at home.

Doughty: *Are you referring to the question of gender?*

Bondar: Somewhat. At school, the girls may be afraid to speak up and the boys aren't. But even if you have equality at school, if a girl goes home and is told to help her mother with the dishes and get a job as a secretary, it's a big problem.

Doughty: *Do you think social values are now more conservative?*

Bondar: You're exactly right. It's like a cultural whiplash. Maybe it's because there are a lot of single parents or two-income families that kids are craving traditional values. Still, I know in my heart of hearts that teachers can give both boys and girls so much strength that they can go home, receive mixed messages, and retain a love of learning no matter what.

Doughty: *How have you seen the pattern emerging across Canada?*

Bondar: In some parts of our country people have tremendous resources and in others they are just starved for information. I don't think that we should have that inequality in our country. I think people should have equal access to information and to exciting things. But, I'm afraid we are getting very splintered in terms of education.

Doughty: *Any solutions?*

Bondar: I don't have any. But I do know that we need co-operation among the provinces, some way of identifying issues and some way of spreading wealth. I'm on Premier Peterson's Council on Science and Technology and I try to have an effect. I also know that the Premiers and the Deputy Ministers meet, but I don't know what they do. What I do know is that when I go out to speak to a small community, I find that there is a great deal that these people have to offer. There are wonderful minds in Canada.

Doughty: *And the future?*

Bondar: Things have changed so much in the past 20 years: computers at work; VCRs at home. We need basic education just to survive. I'm not a genius. I'm not going to go out and join Mensa, but I know that science is something that the average person can enjoy. I think it has to be represented in a fun way, in a way that is relevant to the individual. If a child can go home and say: "Hey, mom!" or "Hey, dad!" and explain what they've learned, then they own that. They *own* that for the rest of their lives. And that is the best we can want and the best we can hope for.

RESPONSE

1. How did Roberta Bondar's family contribute to her education?
2. What do you think of Bondar's statement: "At school, the girls may be afraid to speak up and the boys aren't"?

3. Do you agree with Bondar that "science is something that the average person can enjoy"? Explain.

EXTENSION

4. What are you learning in science that helps you in your daily life?
5. In groups, compile a list of things you would like to study in science and present that list to your science teacher.

THE UNSINKABLE VICKI KEITH

NORA McCABE

- In groups, describe something which you have accomplished which has given you a sense of pride.

L ast August 30 at 6:03 A.M. precisely, marathon swimmer Vicki Keith touched terra firma at Toronto's Leslie Street Spit. When she climbed out of the cold water of Lake Ontario — shivering, dazed and bloated after 23 hours and 38 minutes in the water — she became the first person to swim across all five Great Lakes.

"I'd just done something that no one else in the world has ever done — something that everybody told me was impossible," Keith recalls, the thrill of her achievement echoing in her voice months later. "And when I walked out of that water, I felt fantastic. I'd been throwing up for the last 10 hours. Every muscle in my body hurt. I had stomach cramps. I had cramps in almost every part of my body. And you know what? I never felt better in my life."

Conquering all the Great Lakes in one lifetime, never mind a single summer, is a prodigious feat. Keith's history-making aquatic odyssey did more than make the 28-year-old swimmer eligible for the *Guinness Book of Records* and create an instant celebrity. It shattered the perceived limits of physical pain and mental agony.

Consider exactly what Keith did last summer. Between July 1, when she plunged into Lake Erie, and August 30, when she climbed out of Lake Ontario, she covered a distance of 275 kilometres.

On July 19, she became the first person to cross Lake Huron — an enervating 47-hour trip, during which she spent most of the second night trapped in a world of watery fatigue-induced hallucinations. Even with the shoreline in sight, the final hours were a supreme test of mind over matter. For 90 minutes, her only goal was to force each arm to continue stroking. Over and over, she chanted, "Okay, right arm go, okay, left arm go." Then, realizing she would indeed make land, she began to swim faster, and finished the last kilometre in the punishing butterfly.

Six days and 23 hours after this, defying conventional wisdom that there should be several weeks' rest between marathons, she walked into Lake Michigan's 2.5-metre waves. All day, she swam in 38°C heat. At night, she was attacked by bugs that bit into the raw patches on her arms and shoulders where her skin had peeled from sunburn. Undaunted, she swam on. She completed the final one-and-a-half kilometres of the 53-hour crossing in 24 minutes — her second fastest time ever.

On August 15, Keith scored another first. She conquered Lake Superior, swimming the last seven hours in 12°C water that numbed her hands to the point where she couldn't hold her fingers together. Her face, she says, was frozen into a grin. She couldn't feel her legs when she finally staggered up on shore. But she had beaten the lake. "Call it Lake Inferior," she gloated.

The last lake was Ontario. Having completed a nonstop two-way crossing on August 7, 1987, a 56-hour trek considered one of the last major marathon-swim frontiers, Keith needed to add "a little twist" to keep up her interest. So, she swam the first 38 kilometres of the 51-kilometre crossing in the butterfly — in the process obliterating her own 19-kilometre record set in 1985.

What Vicki Keith did so transcends the normal expectations of athletic achievement as to be incomprehensible; downright freakish, in fact. Concurrent with the feeling of awe aroused by her monumental drive comes a feeling of dismay at her self-inflicted ordeal.

Does Keith herself think people view her as some kind of freak, an aberration to provide jaded sports fans with a new kick?

"I don't think so," she says. "People now are really into the endurance-type sports. They see the challenge, the fight — with yourself, with the elements — making it through adversity. Nobody comes up to you and says, 'Wow! You're a freak.'

"And I'm not. I'm just like everybody else. I'm an average human being who's found something I really enjoy doing, that I'm good at."

Finding what she was good at wasn't easy at first. These days, she likes to tell self-deprecating stories about what a klutz she was athletically before she discovered judo, then competitive swimming. Born in Winnipeg on February 26, 1961, she was the second of four children and the only girl. She was a pigeon-toed, nearsighted headstrong child who learned to swim at age 5. When she was 16, the family moved to Kingston, Ont., where her mother, Carol, who was a competitive swimmer in her youth, is now a nurse, and her father, Brian, an engineer with the Urban Transportation Development Corporation.

Vicki's willingness to take on the elements developed early. At 10, on a dare, she jumped into the frigid water at the family cottage on Thanksgiving Day, waterskied around the lake, then got out and ate an ice-cream bar. As she grew older, she became a lifeguard and swim coach, then dropped out of a psychology course at Queen's University in Kingston, Ont., to train as a marathon swimmer. Coaching allowed her to train five hours daily once her marathon plans developed.

The idea of turning the sports world on its ear with a series of marathon swims came to her one night in 1979 when she was 18. She did not start training seriously until 1984. Then, within three months, she set her first two world records: the 19-kilometre butterfly and the 100-hour continuous swim.

Today, Keith has a well-padded 5-foot-5 ³/₄-inch frame that is best described as stocky. She has been called a motivated water mammal and owns more than 280 stuffed penguins. She preaches the gospel that nothing is impossible if you want it badly enough: believe in yourself and reach for your dreams. She's saved from being a bore by her sense of humor. "I guess I'm gullible. I believe everything I tell myself."

Actually, when Keith, a lover of sun and heat, enters the frigid waters of a large lake, clad only in goggles, a skimpy Speedo suit, two bathing caps and a liberal coating of lanolin, she performs a mental sleight of hand. By focusing on her goal, she tunes out cold and pain. Because she is a purist, she won't relieve the monotony by listening to a submersible Walkman, as she does when training, so she plays mental games or thinks up funny lines to amuse the crew of the powerboats that accompany her. To replenish her energy and lost body weight, every two hours she eats hot chocolate, fruit cocktail, soup and cookies. The crew often includes her parents and friends. Though currently between boyfriends, Keith does find time for a private life between swims, and enjoys movies with her friends or shopping for clothes, preferably with a penguin motif.

Oddly enough, Keith never expected to become famous, and it was not until she completed the double crossing of Lake Ontario that she became a national news item. "When I started, I thought I was doing something for myself. Between the double cross and the Great Lakes swim, I decided I could be a role model." So, these days, having quit her job as a swim coach last spring, Keith, who moved to Toronto in November, supports herself by giving pep talks to business and service groups and to schoolchildren.

At the Oakridge Junior Public School in east-end Toronto, Keith is introduced to 300 students as "the first national hero ever to come to Oakridge." The children are agog as she recounts her summer odyssey. Afterward, they give her a cheque for $400 — money they raised themselves to help Keith's fund-raising efforts for the $5.8-million aquatic wing for disabled youth at Variety Village.

But at an IBM awards dinner at Toronto's Sheraton Centre Hotel, where she receives a cheque for $5,000 boosting her Variety Village fund-raising to more than $500,000, the reaction to her is mixed. Many are enthralled. Others observe that as an employee she'd be difficult to manage and as a boss she'd have no sense of moderation.

It's clear that Vicki Keith is haunted by fear of failing, what she calls "messing up." Underneath her flippant quip that she became a marathon swimmer "because Everest is too far away" lies the need to keep on proving "I can accomplish anything I want in swimming."

Now that she's licked five lakes, what's next? Exactly what task she plans for this year she won't reveal until the logistics are worked out. However, there are still marathon swims to be swum. And Vicki Keith will tackle them. Because she has to. Besides, as she's fond of saying, "I think people want to be amazed."

RESPONSE

1. What do you think of Vicki Keith's achievements?
2. Discuss your feelings about these statements made by Vicki Keith:
   a) "I'm just like everybody else."
   b) ". . . I'm gullible. I believe everything I tell myself."
   c) "I can accomplish anything I want in swimming."
   d) "I think people want to be amazed."

EXTENSION

3. a) Identify a goal which you wish to achieve.
   b) List the obstacles which you perceive may prohibit you from attaining that goal.
   c) List the specific ways in which you might overcome those obstacles.
4. Discuss the qualities, other than physical, that are required for such an accomplishment. How can you acquire and develop these qualities?

POLAR DARE

PRISCILLA TURNER

- Do you enjoy solitude?
- What do you think are the benefits of solitude?
- What is the difference between loneliness and solitude?

The fourth polar bear was Helen Thayer's biggest problem. On her way to the North Magnetic Pole in April 1988, Thayer had already persuaded three of the giant hunters to go off and look for an unwary seal, rather than eat her and her obnoxious flares. But the fourth bear was not the subtle type. He charged from behind an iceberg, went for her 160-pound sled, flipped it, and started toward her.

"In that moment I realized that all I had learnt meant nothing," says Thayer, a petite 51-year-old climbing guide from Snohomish, Washington, "that in the face of that magnificent, killing creature, my gun might as well have been a toothpick and that I was no more important than the tiniest speck of snow. I knew if he got my head in his mouth, there'd be a very loud crunch."

Never mind cold so bitter it shattered canisters of film, winds that knocked Thayer flat, and the eerie feeling of navigating on sea ice out of sight of land. The worst thing about Thayer's 345-mile, 27-day trek were the bears, who move silently on thick padded paws and rarely come across anything on the ice that isn't a potential meal. Helen had expected to face them all by herself. But before she left her base camp on Cornwallis Island in Canada's Northwest Territories, an Inuit polar bear hunter gave her a guard dog, a big, black Husky/Newfoundland whom she named Charlie.

It was Charlie who staved off the terminal crunch. As the fourth bear lowered for his charge, Thayer released the dog, who grabbed the bear by a hind leg and started him spinning like a furry planet. The huge beast took off as soon as he could. Charlie followed in rabid fury, leaving Helen to consider what it would have been like to make her trek absolutely, completely alone.

In spite of the bears, Helen Thayer eventually became the first woman — and one of just two people in recent history — to ski solo to the North Magnetic Pole. The remarkable thing about her achievement is that she made it without the back-up of sled dogs, snowmobiles, or major sponsorship. This sets her apart from many recent polar expeditions backed by large networks and lots of money.

Perhaps the most extreme contrast to Thayer is the Japanese film star who headed for the North Pole with guides and a small flotilla of snowmobiles as a publicity stunt. She never made it. Even more seasoned and respected adventurers have taken comforts where they could. When Frenchman Jean-Louis Etienne skied to the true North Pole in 1986, his crew flew in everything from sleds to soap on five separate occasions. A woman friend dropped by for a visit, bringing smoked salmon that his stomach couldn't abide after simpler camp food.

As Thayer skied steadily north toward her goal, she left prime bear territory behind, but not the cold facts of traveling in the High Arctic. In temperatures as low as minus 48 degrees Fahrenheit, elastic straps stretched out and never snapped back, and frost formed on Thayer's eyelashes. Violent storms confined her to her tent for up to five days at a time. Once her fingers were so cold she used her elbows to set up her stove, and nearly burned down her tent.

And there were the smaller idiosyncrasies of Arctic life: Thayer let Charlie eat out of her dish after his got banged up and blew away; she didn't change her clothes for 27 days; she had to slit the hem of her jacket to release ice formed from frozen condensation. And she had to make sure that her diary, logbook and exposed film were stowed in separate parts of her gear — if a bear got her and thrashed through her supplies, there might be at least some hope of recovering a partial record of the expedition.

Thayer threw herself at the High Arctic with very little margin for error. Her "crew" consisted of an Arctic outfitter in Resolute, Cornwallis Island, Canada, who listened for her radio reports every night, and her 61-year-old husband, Bill, a pilot who would have gone with her if there'd been enough money. Instead, he went to Florida and dusted crops to help cover the expedition's $10,000 cost. Thayer was so broke at the end of the trip that she couldn't afford to have her sled freighted back home with her.

Helen Thayer does not like to talk about fear, even though she's spent a lifetime facing it. She's survived expeditions when others have been lost, but she's as unwilling to talk about these tragedies as she is to linger over her accomplishments. And those are considerable: since her fortieth birthday, she has climbed both the highest mountain in North America, Alaska's 20,300-foot Mt. Denali, and the tallest in the Soviet Union, 24,500-foot Peak Communism. This says nothing of previous exploits on the high volcanoes of Mexico and South America.

If you press her about the trials of her adventures, she'll change the subject to the family she met when she was climbing in the Pamir Range of Central Asia. She left the rest of her party, hiked 14 miles down to an idyllic valley and spent the night in a dirt-floored *yurt* with a Tadzhik clan. "We didn't speak each other's language," Thayer says, "but the teenage daughter cried when she saw me getting ready to go."

Like many other accomplished climbers and adventurers, Thayer would rather discuss "working through fear" than the great panicky abyss itself. She considers a terrifying situation a set of problems that must be solved on a very tight deadline. "I just figure out what the steps are," she says with the discipline of a soldier or an athlete, "and get the job done. If it doesn't have to do with the thing before me, I don't let myself think about it." Perhaps it's this unwillingness to ponder the ultimate consequences that saves Thayer's neck. Consider the time, near the end of her expedition, when a sudden catastrophe just about did her in.

Storms in the High Arctic usually are not blizzards. Thayer remembers how strange it was to see the sun burning in a blue sky overhead, when the temperature dropped to 20 or 30 degrees below zero and airborne ice crystals glazed the horizon. Not much snow falls in these icy, arid reaches, but the winds, with nothing to stop them, shoot along at speeds exceeding 75 miles per hour.

"These storms would blow up out of nowhere," explains Thayer. "You barely have time to react." One afternoon, Thayer had just stopped to set up her tent for shelter, when a sudden blast blew by her, taking with it much of her food and fuel. She reached out and grabbed what she could, miraculously snaring Charlie's chow. Then a sideways gust knocked Thayer over, jarring loose her goggles. As she turned to see how Charlie was faring, the wind drove ice crystals into her right eye, virtually blinding her. Thayer managed to reach Charlie and huddle with him behind her sled for about two hours, waiting for the winds to dissipate. "Frankly," says Thayer, "I was a little bit worried we'd freeze to death right there."

Eventually the storm subsided and Thayer took inventory. All that remained of her food was a store of walnuts, which she divided into piles, then smaller piles, to gauge how many days of travel the meager supply would support. "You see, I knew I was almost at my goal. There was no point in radioing in and saying 'Come pick me up.' They couldn't have even if I'd wanted them to. I had to get to the place where I knew they could land," explains Thayer.

In spite of her injured eye and paltry rations, Thayer kept on traveling toward, around, and possibly even over the North Magnetic Pole. Unlike the true pole, the North Magnetic Pole does not sit benignly at the top of the world. Some 600 miles to the south, it wanders like a refugee, roughly scribing an ellipse that may vary from 40 to 150 miles in a single day, depending upon magnetic disturbances deep under the earth's surface. Thayer covered the entire North Magnetic Pole area; she used her watch, sun tables and the sun itself to navigate because magnetic forces in these remote regions render compasses useless.

For several days, she couldn't see well enough to make out her charts, so she relied on the pathfinding method Inuits have been using for years, following the *sastrugi*, the long wavelike ridges in the ice formed by prevailing winds. "And when I couldn't see those, I just went by the feel of the wind on my shoulder," she says.

By the time the five-foot-three-inch former discus thrower and sled racer reached her pickup point on Helena Island, she was dead sure she'd nailed the North Magnetic Pole. Then she warmed the batteries for her radio against her ribs, extended the 100-foot aerial and called for a plane to come pick her up. The pilot, who arrived the next day, gave Thayer his sandwich (for a week she'd been telling Charlie that he might just have to start sharing his chow). Thayer kept something else the pilot had given her — a $1,623 bill that she believes will save her from the fate of Rear Admiral Robert Peary, whose dubious record keeping was recently called into question. The bill certifies that Thayer has actually been to the North Magnetic Pole.

Thayer has always loved what she calls "the outdoor lifestyle." As a farm girl growing up near Auckland, New Zealand, she ran her first race at age five, and climbed 8,400-foot Mt. Egmont four years later. Before long, climbing acquaintances had introduced her to Edmund Hillary, a fellow New Zealander and pioneer Everest climber who quickly became one of Thayer's heroes.

In high school she embarked upon a 15-year track and field career, which led her to throw discus in international competition for New Zealand, the United States, and Guatemala, where she and her husband settled soon after their marriage nearly 30 years ago.

Back in the U.S. the Thayers eventually bought a dairy farm in the foothills of Washington State's Cascade Mountains, a convenient base for frequent climbing trips. After watching a luge race on television one day in 1972, Thayer decided that charging down an icy course on a sled with primitive steering might just be her kind of sport. Within two years, she was the U.S. national champion, and a strong contender for the 1976 U.S. Olympic team. But the lure of the mountains was too strong. Thayer gave up the luge and started climbing in the higher altitudes, earning a reputation as one of the Pacific Northwest's top women climbers.

Though she hopes to scale Mt. Denali once more before the decade is out, Thayer hasn't finished exploring the Arctic yet. The North Magnetic Pole trip was just a warm-up. Thayer and her husband, Bill, plan to make an expedition to the true North Pole next year; they are determined to do it without re-supply or backup of any sort. If they're successful, they hope to tackle the South Pole next.

In the meantime, Thayer isn't losing any ground. She does hour-long workouts on a homemade weight set every morning at five

A.M., hauls a sled up the steep wooded hills behind the corral where she keeps five amiable goats, and squeezes in a daily 10-mile run with her faithful friend Charlie, who is still learning the ropes of living in a house. The first time Thayer left him alone at home, he tried to chew his way through the kitchen door. But that was nothing compared to his reaction when he saw the image of a polar bear during one of Thayer's slide shows. "He did his rabid-dog routine," explains Thayer. "He wouldn't let me near the screen."

There were days during Thayer's epic trek when travel went so smoothly that her trip was the grand adventure such things are meant to be. Daylight lingers almost 24 hours in a High Arctic April. When Thayer found flat ice, she could ski as far as 35 miles a day, each mile an easy victory after the boulders and ditches of garbaged ice. It was then — in moments of diminished danger and adversity — that Thayer let down her customary guard.

She remembers one afternoon when she saw a commercial jet on its way over the North Pole. She stopped and explained to Charlie, who had never seen a green field, a cat, or a dandelion, that people up there were eating fine, hot food and sitting in plush seats. She stood still for a long time, her eyes following the plane across the open sky until it flew over the top of the world.

RESPONSE

1. What do you think Helen Thayer means by "working through fear"?
2. What is the most exceptional aspect of Thayer's personality as far as you are concerned?
3. What events in Thayer's life made her adventure more understandable?

EXTENSION

4. Write an account of the most exciting thing you have ever done.
5. Discuss with your group how a person can live an interesting and fulfilling life without accepting any really dangerous challenges.

GREG LeMOND'S GREATEST RACE

E.M. SWIFT

- In your journal, write about what you consider to be your greatest achievement.
- What did you have to give up in order to realize this accomplishment?

I t was a ride the experts believed simply couldn't be done. Not with the Tour de France, cycling's most prestigious race, on the line. Certainly not by Greg LeMond, the American whose body was still riddled with lead shotgun pellets.

The distance of the final stage from Versailles to Paris (24.5 kilometres) was too short; the time to make up (50 seconds) too great. And Laurent Fignon, the two-time Tour winner and overall leader, was too arrogant to be whipped on his home turf by an American in 1989, the bicentennial year of the French Revolution.

"Greg believes he can win," Fignon said on the eve of the last time trial. "But it is impossible. I am too strong in the mind and the legs."

Not even LeMond's most optimistic supporters believed the 28-year-old could erase Fignon's lead — not even his wife, Kathy. To her, *le maillot jaune*, the famous yellow jersey awarded the leader at each stage of the race, did not matter. Second place would be miracle enough.

LeMond started competitive cycling in 1976 at age 14 in the hills around Reno, Nevada. He ascended in his sport at a dizzying pace, turning pro at 19, joining a top French team and establishing himself among cycling's elite. In 1983, LeMond became the first North American ever to win the professional road race at the world championships. Then, in 1986, at 25, he became the first non-European ever to win the Tour de France. With his prime years still ahead of him, Greg was at the top of the heap.

All that changed in April 1987 when LeMond went hunting with his brother-in-law on a ranch in Lincoln, California. Settled behind a bush, Greg heard a shotgun blast and instantly felt the blow of 60 No. 2-sized pellets fired accidentally into his back and side. LeMond could barely breathe — his right lung had collapsed, and his kidney, liver, diaphragm and intestine were hit. Two pellets lodged in the lining of the walls of his heart.

Waiting for a rescue helicopter, Greg wasn't worried if he would ride again; he wondered: *Will I live to see my wife and kids?*

Miraculously, none of the damage was irreparable, though not all the pellets could be removed. Eight weeks later LeMond started training again. But every time he started to show signs of progress, something would set him back.

Four months after the accident an emergency appendectomy ended his 1987 season. In July 1988 surgery to repair an infected shin tendon forced him to miss the Tour de France again.

The powerful Dutch team PDM, with which LeMond had signed a two-year deal in 1987, lost confidence in him.

But LeMond kept training. He knew he had to allow his body time to recuperate. Still, when he read what sceptics were saying, he kept hearing a voice in his head: *Maybe you'll never come back.*

Lowest Point. Before the start of the 1989 season, LeMond took a pay cut and signed with ADR, a Belgian company. ADR's lower expectations meant less pressure on Greg.

After riding in the spring classics in Europe, LeMond returned to the United States in May and finished a disappointing 27th in the inaugural Tour de Trump — a New York City race he had designs on winning.

Later that month LeMond faltered again. Before the accident he had been a daunting mountain cyclist. Now he lost more than eight minutes to the leader in the first mountain stage of the Tour of Italy.

His doctor diagnosed anemia and gave him an injection of iron, but the worst was still to come. In the 13th stage of the Tour of Italy, LeMond finished more than 17 minutes behind the leader. That night he called Kathy and told her, "If things don't turn around, I'm quitting at the end of the year." She didn't try to talk him out of it. It was the lowest point in his cycling career.

Shortly after that call, however, LeMond started feeling stronger. In the final stage of the Tour of Italy he decided he'd hold nothing back. If he ran out of energy — "blew up," in cycling parlance — so be it. But LeMond didn't blow up. Instead, he finished second.

So he came to the 76th Tour de France quietly hopeful. His goals for the celebrated 23-day, 3273-kilometre race were to finish in the top 20 overall and to win one of the 21 stages.

With its supercharged atmosphere, the throngs of people lining the roads and the live TV coverage, the Tour de France is an event unlike any other, and LeMond felt invigorated. In the July 1 Prologue — a 7.8-kilometre opening sprint against the clock — his morale got a further boost when he finished fourth among 198 starters, nearly tied with Fignon. *If I can finish in the top five there,* he thought, *I can finish in the top five overall.*

Taking the Yellow Jersey. His first major test came during the fifth stage, a 73-kilometre time trial through Brittany. The cyclists, spaced at one- to two-minute intervals, go all out against the clock. LeMond rode like the LeMond of old, catching five of the riders who had started ahead of him and covering the rain-swept course at an average speed of about 45 kilometres an hour. He beat defending champion Pedro Delgado of Spain by 24 seconds, and Fignon by 56 seconds.

The margin of LeMond's victory propelled him into first place in the overall standings, five seconds ahead of arch rival Fignon. Clutching the yellow jersey, LeMond began thinking that he might just be able to win the whole darn thing. But the mountains were still to come, and he hadn't raced well there for three years.

Once in the Pyrenees, however, LeMond stayed with Fignon the entire 147 kilometres of the first mountainous stage, and hung on to the yellow jersey for a fourth straight day.

On the second and last day in the Pyrenees, Fignon attacked. And on the final climb, an 18-kilometre monster, instead of keeping his pace and gradually recovering ground, LeMond caught up too quickly. It was a tactical error. Suddenly LeMond blew up, putting his body into oxygen debt. In the last 800 metres Fignon gained 12 seconds on him to take over the yellow jersey.

Privately, LeMond believed it was to his advantage that Fignon had the jersey. Now Fignon would be expected to control each day's stage, chasing down attackers. LeMond, just seven seconds back, felt the pressure ease.

The next three stages resulted in few changes in the overall standings. Then on July 16, with only a week to go, LeMond recaptured the yellow jersey. He beat Fignon by 47 seconds in the first of four gruelling days in the Alps. Fignon lost another 13 seconds to LeMond in the 16th stage, a 174-kilometre route from Gap to Briançon that included a tortuous 20-kilometre climb up the Col d'Izoard.

The next day, more than halfway up the 1860-metre-high, 15-kilometre-long climb on L'Alpe d'Huez, the Tour's single most difficult ascent, LeMond began running out of energy. Fignon bolted past him and once again took the yellow jersey. LeMond now trailed Fignon by 26 seconds, a margin Fignon enlarged the next day to 50 seconds.

The experts believed the race was over. The best LeMond could hope for was to gain one second per kilometre or so in the final time trial into Paris — maybe 25 seconds in all — half the time he needed for a win. "You raced a great race, Greg," Fignon told LeMond. "My coach predicted that this is the way it would finish, me winning and you second."

LeMond thanked him. But he was thinking: *It's not over yet, pal. You're not psyching me into quitting.*

Head Down, All Out. The way LeMond had it figured, his race had already been won. He had proved wrong all those who said: You can't; you don't have the strength or desire. He had even vanquished his worst enemy, the inner voice that had tried, in the darkest moments, to convince him to give up. Fignon and the 50 seconds were a last golden apple to reach for. The important matter had been settled. LeMond no longer doubted himself.

There was a festive air about Paris on July 23. LeMond felt terrific. In the morning he took a practice ride on the final course to get a feel for it. His plan: to keep his head down and ride as fast as he could.

Fignon took off two minutes behind LeMond. Inexplicably, Fignon had discarded his racing helmet and let his ponytail flap in the breeze, a triumph of vanity over aerodynamics. After five kilometres Fignon's coach shouted to him that he had lost ten seconds. Fignon cranked up his pace. After ten kilometres he had lost 19 seconds. After 18 kilometres, 35 seconds. Fignon couldn't believe it. Harder and harder he rode, panic creeping into his legs.

LeMond, meanwhile, had no notion of the stir he was creating until he reached the Champs-Elysées, about five kilometres from the finish. Heading towards the Arc de Triomphe, LeMond thought he heard an announcer say he had gained 40 seconds on Fignon. He crossed the finish line in a record 26 minutes, 57 seconds.

Now there was nothing to do but wait.

LeMond glanced at the ticking digital clock and knew the outcome would be close. He could make out Fignon now, wearing the yellow jersey, barrelling towards the finish. Watching the clock, then Fignon, LeMond kept thinking how terrible it would be to lose by one second after more than 3200 kilometres.

Then that second quietly passed . . . 27:47 . . . 27:48 . . . He had won. Fignon crossed the line and slid from his bike, collapsing in exhaustion. His time: 27:55 — third best of the day. Incredibly, it was 58 seconds slower than LeMond's. Fignon held his head in his hands. LeMond had averaged 54.7 kilometres an hour — the fastest time trial ever in the Tour de France.

On the victory podium LeMond thought back over the last two years with wonder. He had almost quit two months before. But now the race's outcome reinforced what he had known all long: *Never* give up.

In July 1990, Greg LeMond won — for a third time — the Tour de France. He is the first non-European to accomplish the feat.

RESPONSE

1. If you were Greg LeMond, which of the obstacles he faced would you have the most difficulty overcoming?
2. What aspects of Greg LeMond's character do you admire the most?

EXTENSION

3. Investigate the course of the Tour de France and present your findings to the class.
4. Imagine you are Fignon on the last day of the Tour de France. Write a journal account of the events of that day.

JOHNNY BIOSPHERE TO THE RESCUE

PETER GORRIE

- Think of a cause or issue in which you believe strongly, and explain why you think it is important.
- Would other people's reactions lead you to stop advocating this cause? Explain.

W henever Jack Vallentyne travels more than 10 kilometres from his home in Burlington, Ontario, he takes along the same three items — a brown safari suit, high-cut running shoes, and a globe with a battery-powered light strapped to the top of a knapsack.

The outfit was designed to attract the attention of students when, in 1980, Vallentyne devised his alter ego, Johnny Biosphere, and began visiting schools to talk about the importance of saving the Great Lakes and the rest of earth's environment.

Now he wears the apparatus almost everywhere. "If I go into a tavern and start flashing the light, I get quite a reaction," Vallentyne says with a chuckle.

Occasionally, those he encounters pronounce him goofy. But Vallentyne, 64, is a highly respected scientist at the federal government's Canada Centre for Inland Waters in Burlington, and Canadian co-chairman of the International Joint Commission's Science Advisory Board. He uses Johnny Biosphere as a part of a carefully considered mission: making himself conspicuous to help spread the message that humans must adopt new ways of thinking and acting if the biosphere — the thin layer of land, air, and water inhabited by all living things — is to continue to support life.

Vallentyne makes frequent presentations to scientific conferences and other adult groups. However, he says students are his most important audience. As Johnny Biosphere, he has visited hundreds of schools around the world, presenting "60 action-packed minutes of ecological fun and games with a deadly serious message," illustrated with items from his bulging knapsack.

A tape-recorder produces wolf howls, moose and loon calls, and rumbling thunder. He sprays vinegar water on a half-dead, potted plant as he discusses the impact of acid rain, and sprinkles potato chips or pop on a flower to make a point about nutrition and food sources. Sometimes he pulls a balloon out of the pack and blows it up until it bursts, to demonstrate the limits of growth.

The message is global, but the focus of Vallentyne's work is the Great Lakes basin — his boyhood and current home and the subject of his most important field studies. Growing up in Brantford, Ontario, in the 1930s, he developed a deep love of nature as he played along the Grand River, which flows into Lake Erie. Forty years later, his research provided conclusive proof that the phosphates in detergent were a major source of the nutrients feeding dense algae blooms then choking the over-enriched lake.

Vallentyne sees the Great Lakes as a world symbol. "The way the lakes are going is how the earth is going," he says. "If we can turn that system around, then maybe the rest of our polluted planet can be saved."

He is hopeful that even Lake Ontario can be made clean enough again for eagles, although getting rid of the toxic chemicals and restoring degraded wildlife habitats might take 100 years.

The water is much cleaner than it was two decades ago, he notes: "The lakes are a turn-around success story." More important, the students he encounters in elementary schools are becoming very aware of environmental problems. "Kids' attitudes have changed more in the past three or four years than they did in the previous century, and they're influencing their parents and the political system," he said.

Vallentyne also predicts humans will realize, before it is too late, that their health, and even their survival, depend on living in balance with the biosphere: "We're a cunning species. We'll get over these troubles before they do us in."

RESPONSE

1. Prove that Jack Vallentyne acts out of hope rather than despair.
2. Why are the Great Lakes so important to Jack Vallentyne's message?

EXTENSION

3. For Discussion: Why does Jack Vallentyne care so demonstratively about the Great Lakes and the rest of the biosphere?

I USED TO PLAY BASS IN A BAND

SANDRA BIRDSELL

- Approximately four out of every ten high school students do not graduate. Why do you think they leave school? What do you think happens to students who do not graduate?
- Do you think those who graduate are responsible for those who don't? Explain.

I met Terry this summer one sweltering night as I sat out on the deck visiting with a friend. I had been away from Winnipeg for two years and Roger, who operates a travel agency in the area, summarized the changes in the neighbourhood. The neighbourhood: the rubbing of shoulders on Westminster Avenue of professional people along with the indigent natives and the poor on their way to the Agape Table, the funky and most of the city's artists, all living within several blocks in an area in Winnipeg which is referred to as the "Granola Belt."

Sounds from the front street echoed between the houses, the sounds of parties in the making in the clink of empty bottles inside beer cartons. A person riding a bicycle darted by in the lane and I saw the flash of long copper-coloured hair as the rider passed through the light of the streetlamp. "And then there's Terry," my friend sang softly under his breath and was about to say more when we heard the sound of tires skidding as the bicycle came to a halt. Terry, straddling the bicycle, walked backwards into view and stopped beside a pile of boxes across the lane. Their contents, the remainder of a garage sale held earlier in the day, had already attracted much attention. One of our lawn chairs may have squeaked or perhaps the movement was as minute as the blink of an eye, but Terry sensed our presence and veered away from the stack of cartons. Roger called a greeting and then explained that Terry often dropped by the agency to browse but more than often to talk his ear off.

Terry shielded his eyes against the glare of the streetlamp and peered into the yard. Then he stood up and simply walked free of his bicycle, letting it drop to the ground. He appeared to be all limbs and had the awkward lope of a young animal as he entered the yard, calling his greeting in breathless run-on sentences.

"Rog, hey Rog, how're you doing, eh? Haven't seen you in ages, man, how've you been? I checked out your lead? Medi Equip? Wanted me to work in a spray booth. No ventilation, just masks, eh. I told them no way. I'm not putting my lungs on the line for the minimum. So, how you been, eh?" His voice has a disarming quality to it, yet urgent too. Like that of a cat entering a yard in the morning after a long night of prowling and not being able to decide whether it wants to be fed or fondled.

Roger introduced us. I was intrigued by the contradictions in Terry's appearance: the suggestion of fragility in his much-too-thin body, the audacious "screw the world" kind of message on his tee-shirt which belied the tremor of vulnerability in his anxious smile. The tilt of his khaki beret, the stylish paisley scarf knotted at his waist, were at odds with his scuffed and almost shapeless cowboy boots. A knapsack dangled at his side. He towered above us, casting a lean shadow across the lawn. He was like the street, I thought. A combination of all the people who passed by my house.

"Your soffits are rotting," he said. "If you don't get them replaced you'll end up with water damage in the ceilings on the second floor." He said he couldn't help but notice the loose boards each time he passed by. I didn't know whether to be annoyed or grateful for the information. I sensed Roger's uneasiness when I invited Terry to join us and offered him a cold drink.

When I returned from the house, Terry had helped himself to a cigarette from Roger's package and jostled a handful of nuts he'd scooped from the bowl on the table. Beside the bowl was a pamphlet. He said it was for me, that he wasn't in the business, not to worry, eh. He wasn't trying to sell me anything but in his estimation, this company's line of roofing supplies was the best. He liked my house, he said; like all the houses in the neighbourhood, it had character. I asked him if he lived in the area, then, but instead of answering, he shifted in his chair suddenly and pointed out a garage across the street. "Used to be a livery stable, far out," he said and did we know that once all the houses along here burned coal? "Fossil fuel, imagine," he said. "I can imagine the shapes of fossils drifting up the chimneys."

"Aha," I said in answer. Not long ago when I had gone walking in the night I had passed by a young woman with a dreamy, serene smile. She'd said good evening and then warned me to take care because the cats were flying in the sky. I said aha then, too.

Terry stooped to rummage in the knapsack planted between his feet. "Picked this up today," he said. The book was a colourful compact guide to fossils, the kind often sold in museum gift shops. He thumbed through it. I asked him if he was interested in geology.

"Adapt or die," he said, "except for the cockroach. Paleontology is the study of fossils," he read. "Yeah, I'm interested." He closed the book and placed it on the table in front of him. "You know the painting, *Starry Night*?" he asked. He'd seen it in a retrospective of Vincent van Gogh and what he'd really like to do, he said, was paint like that. "Instead of stars," he said and nudged at the book with a long bony finger, "I'd like to paint the sky full of trilobites swimming in a tropical forest." I told him I had once lined up for half a day outside a gallery in Paris to see the painting in a show of van Gogh's work and I thought it was impossible to improve on a van Gogh sky. "Oh wow," he said, "you've seen it? Oh wow." He shook his head at the wonder of it. So was he, Terry, an artist, then?

"Yeah," he said with the same nervous shift in his body. "That and music, eh. I used to play bass in a band." I tried not to smile. I thought his statement would make a great title for a story. "I used to play bass in a band" neatly summed up the lives of several young people I had met recently.

Terry set his empty glass down on the table between us and leaned forward. "Tell me," he said, "do you think van Gogh was crazy?"

Well, I wondered, hadn't the man been treated by a psychiatrist and for a time confined?

Terry was quiet for several moments. It seemed to me that his sharp features had become less fox-like and softer. "I don't know whether he was or not," he said, "but that's what most people say. That he was crazy. But what I think," he said, "is that when van Gogh painted, he was in a different state of consciousness."

Roger replied wryly, yes, drunk as opposed to sober. Terry's expression grew strained and his voice appealed for our patience, to let him finish what he'd begun to say. "Hey, Rog, no, listen, man." I sensed he was accustomed to being dismissed. "Hey Rog, why do you think there are so many crazy people in the world?" he asked, using the trick of a question to make Roger pay attention and then going on to say what he wanted to say. "Because," he said, "because so-called crazy people can't conform to the common idea of what is reality."

Which was what? Roger wanted to know. "The reality determined by the first scientists," Terry said. "The cause-and-effect guys, everything can be counted and measured. The notion that we live in a rational and predictable universe." There was no way, he said, that scientists would ever be able to construct a working model of the brain where these other realities existed. Van Gogh hadn't been crazy at all. He'd just given in to his own sense of reality. "You know what I think?" he said. His sharp features grew more animated. "I think the reason why we only use such a small part of our brain is because we've adopted a caveman theory on the idea of what is sense and what is nonsense." He tapped his forehead and grinned. "Tunnel thinking," he said. "Van Gogh had an alternate sense of reality. Probably, all artists do."

"You?" Roger asked.

Terry laughed and lifted his slender hands as though to push the notion away. "Hey man, I'm not that stupid," he said. His wide grin lit up his eyes. "What would you say if I told you that I can actually see trilobites in the sky? You'd get nervous and I might end up with a chemically induced sense of your reality. So I tell you that I imagine I see them. Adapt or die," he said. "There's no way I'm cutting off my ear, man."

We stood on the sidewalk in front of the house. Terry said he wanted to check out the buskers in the Village. In the light of the streetlamp his face appeared pinched and rather pale. I noticed that his teeth were pitted with decay. He pushed off and joined the flow of traffic, the music, the other cyclists. Roger explained that he'd begun to see Terry in early spring. That Terry had slept in a bus shelter on the corner and, he suspected now that it was warmer, along the river bank. "Alternative sense of reality," he said and laughed. "Where does he get those things?" He added that he didn't believe Terry to be a user of drugs.

While the noise of a full-blown party doesn't bother me, I am often awakened in the night by the small sounds, footsteps in the back lane or the creak of a gate. I lay awake listening to the sound of stealth, someone rummaging through the boxes across the lane. I went to the window and saw Terry standing below in the light of the streetlamp. He was without a shirt now and I could see the outline of his ribs beneath his shallow chest. He cradled a book in his hands and turned the pages carefully, as if it were a delicate object. He stopped paging then and stood as though transfixed, leaning into the text. I watched, mesmerized by his intense concentration, a spell cast, and I was unable to move away. The neighbourhood, I, and the night became invisible as we stood, holding our breaths outside of Terry's world.

RESPONSE

1. Demonstrate that Terry's behaviour is consistent with his statement, "Adapt or die."

EXTENSION

2. In groups, discuss what Terry is actually revealing about himself when he says, "I used to play bass in a band."
3. a) If you had chosen not to come to school today, what would you have done?
   b) If you had chosen to drop out of school this morning, what would you have done with the rest of the day?

UNIT 4

RE~ASSESSMENTS

GET REAL!

JUDI BAILEY

- Do you think it is possible to control your emotions? Explain.
- List the ways some people use to avoid dealing with emotions.

Every time Holly feels the least twinge of hurt or rejection, she stuffs herself with cookies, chips, or french fries.

Rather than trying to work through conflicts with his parents, Brad slams into his room, jams on the headphones, and buries his anger in hard rock.

Kristen sleeps. When she's grounded, she sleeps. When she's down, she sleeps. When a big exam approaches, she sleeps.

Emotions are often prickly and squiggly, gripping and tripping. We want to run fast and far from unpleasant feelings. Why experience the smouldering swamp of sorrow, the freezing fever of fear, or the agonizing arrow of anger? Why wallow in rejection, stew in self-pity, or sink in loneliness?

An eight-year-old Navaho Indian boy once asked his grandfather why he didn't mind the bitter cold.

"Because it's real," the grandfather said.

That's exactly why we need to experience our emotions — because they're real. When we don't face our feelings honestly, when we try to tuck our emotions away in little boxes, we suffer a worse fate than the direct experience of these emotions in the first place. Emotions always surface. Here is the question: Do we express emotions directly or let them lurk under the surface, waiting to explode later?

Wrong Ways to Cope

Take Jeff for example. He got caught up in a certain image he wanted to portray. He patterned himself after his hero, Dad: tough, strong, macho, perfect. Jeff believed nothing rattled Dad.

So whenever one of his classmates insulted him, Jeff blew it off. When his dog got hit by a truck, he acted like it was no big deal. When his girlfriend Claudia broke up with him, Jeff said, "Hey, there are lots of girls dying to go out with this dude."

But there weren't. Claudia broke it off because Jeff was so cold. Kids began avoiding him because of his hard attitude. Jeff noticed this rejection, and although he felt lonely and depressed about it, he continued to shove his feelings deep down inside. The stronger they became, the harder he worked at keeping them down. The cycle made him appear even harder and colder, and he grew more and more depressed.

What Jeff couldn't see was that ignoring his depression was just the thing that was keeping him depressed. He also didn't know that his macho father had an ulcer, high blood pressure, headaches, and back pain. Emotions *always* surface in some way.

Stuffing feelings doesn't rid us of discomfort. We can't deposit an emotion safely in some storage unit. It becomes like a sniper slinking across the roof of our hearts waiting to take a shot at us. We can keep the sniper at bay for a while, but eventually he sneaks up on us and lets go with a shot of depression, irritability, laziness, poor grades, fights with friends or parents, physical problems, or other negative factors.

We use a variety of techniques to try stifling unpleasant emotions. Some of us immerse ourselves in junk on TV. Some use alcohol and/or other drugs — then suffer with those effects in addition to the original problems. Others overeat, become obsessed with body building, or live in a world of continual daydreams.

"I thought I had to be all things to all people," says Amy, age 15. "My parents have a lot of their own problems, so I didn't want to burden them with mine. I didn't confide in friends, because I was afraid they'd be disappointed in me, or worse yet, laugh."

So whenever something bothered Amy, she lost herself in a trashy novel. Because she tried so hard not to talk about herself, she began withdrawing from her friends more and more. At home she became irritable with her little brother. At school she used so much energy stuffing her emotions that she had trouble listening in class and concentrating on homework. Finally, a teacher noticed the change in her, pulled her aside, listened to her feelings, and referred her to the school counsellor.

Solutions That Work

• *See the school counsellor.* Sometimes we can't see our situations or ourselves accurately. When this happens, we need an outsider, someone who can objectively view the whole of our circumstances.

"When I first went in to see the counsellor," Amy recalls, "I thought, 'No way am I going to tell my secrets to her!' I was afraid she'd blab all my troubles to the principal and to the other teachers.

But I found out differently. She was someone who took time enough to listen to all my feelings, all my ideas. Then she gave me direction and support. And she treated everything I said as strictly confidential."

Perhaps one or two sessions with your counsellor will be all you need to sort things out or come up with answers to specific problems. Or the counsellor might be someone who can direct you to additional help: a professional counsellor, a school support group, a helpful book.

• *Talk to a friend.* We're surrounded by valuable resources, but how seldom we use them! Friends can be terrific allies when we have frustrating experiences, hurt feelings, or are simply down on ourselves. Having a buddy to get mad *with* you, or to tell you, "I wish you weren't so sad," or to share with you his or her similar circumstances can be the ticket to your relief.

Selecting someone to talk with demands risk, but it means using your head, too. Don't tell your secrets to the school gossip because you hope she'll treat you differently She won't. The story will be school news in no time. And don't choose someone harsh and critical, hoping he'll sympathize with you. He won't. Instead, pick people who listen. It might take some trial and error to find the right ones, but be persistent. Friendships take time, but true friends last.

• *Feel your feelings.* This is the very thing we don't want to do, but what better way to learn about ourselves? So that an emotion doesn't turn into a problem, we first need to acknowledge the emotion. Then we have a chance to do something about it.

How can you deal with your anger if you don't let yourself experience it? How can you get over a rejection if you fool yourself into believing it was "no biggie"?

Yes, it hurts terribly. Yes, you'll wish you hadn't confronted how you feel. Yes, you'll question the purpose of it all. But it works!

Don't confuse this process with dwelling on misfortune or wallowing in self-pity. If someone at practice snubs you, you don't have to reek of rejection for 48 hours. But do check in with yourself, be honest about how you really feel, and allow yourself the privilege of experiencing it. This way it won't sneak out later and express itself in the form of bad language, a physical problem, or a poor performance in band, basketball, or biology.

• *Write things down.* Here's a technique that allows us to experience our feelings and, at the same time, release them.

Writing offers perspective. When we keep information in our heads, we tend to think in a circular pattern. We ponder the same scene, the same hurts, the same revenge over and over again. Writing breaks this circular thinking. We begin at one point and end at another.

Journaling has become a popular tool recommended by mental-health experts. Regularly jotting down thoughts and feelings in a journal, notebook, or diary enables us to understand more clearly the workings of our individual personalities.

You don't have to write every day, but most psychologists encourage notebook entries at least weekly. The more often you write, the more you'll learn and the easier it'll be to use this tool in a crisis.

• *Do physical exercise.* Although it's not solving the problem directly, this is a positive way to work off the excess energy that builds up from our emotions.

Running, walking, aerobics, baseball, basketball, washing the car — any constructive physical exertion — can offer great relief from anger and anxiety. At the same time, it improves health and increases a sense of well-being through the release of amino acids called endorphins.

Be sure to identify your emotion, feel it, and determine what caused it before you release the surplus energy. Don't fall into using physical exercise to *escape* your feelings.

If you feel weak, passive, wimpy, overweight, or have a poor body image, exercise or involvement in a sport might be part of the overall solution.

In addition to the suggestions given here, you may find your own unique ways of handling emotions healthfully. Experiment to find out what works best for you. It could be crying, calling a friend, writing things down, or talking with a favorite aunt or uncle.

Remember that feelings *always* surface. They need to be experienced honestly and directly. Fear needs action; anger needs activity; hurt needs consolation; and loneliness needs acceptance.

Negative feelings are no picnic, but as they say, "The best way around a problem is through it!"

RESPONSE

1. Do you recognize yourself in any of the behaviours of the people mentioned in the first part of Bailey's piece?
2. In groups, evaluate each of the solutions suggested by the author. Develop a solution of your own.
3. "The best way around a problem is through it." Do you think that this statement is valid? Explain.

EXTENSION

4. Compose a letter to "Jeff" advising him about his behaviour toward Claudia and others.
5. Explore the possibility of organizing a peer counselling service in your school. Make recommendations to the school administration.

REMEMBRANCE

TIMOTHY FINDLEY

- In your group, discuss the way you feel about Remembrance Day and its observance.

Today is Remembrance Day, and it's a strange thing to me that we confine ourselves to remembering only the dead — and only the war dead, at that. If they were able, what would *they* be remembering? Us. And we're alive. Here we are. Maybe it's sad — I suppose it is — that the dead should be remembering the living and the living remembering the dead. But the main thing is, we all remember when we were together. We remember what we were in another time. Not now, but *then*. Memory is making peace with time.

They say that loss of memory is not to know who you are. Then, I suppose, it has to follow that we *are* what we remember. I can believe that. I mean, it's very easy for me to imagine forgetting my name. That wouldn't worry me. And it wouldn't worry me to forget how old I am (I wish I could!) or to forget the colour of my eyes and have to go look in a mirror to remind myself. None of that would worry me. Because I can skip all of that. None of those things are who I am.

But it would worry the hell out of me if I couldn't remember the smell of the house where I grew up, or the sound of my father playing the piano, or the tune of his favourite song. I remember my brother, Michael, as a child. And the child I remember being myself is as much a remembrance of him as it is of me. More, in fact — because I saw him every day and did not see myself. I heard him every day — and did not hear myself (except singing). So, to be a child in memory means that I conjure Michael, not the child in photographs who bears my name.

I am my Aunt Marg, for instance, telling me not to lean into the cemetery over the fence at Foxbar Road. I am not me leaning over the fence, I am her voice — because that is what I remember. And I am all the gravestones I was looking at when she called me. And the fence boards that supported me. And the sun on my back. But I am not that little boy. I don't remember him at all. I remember him falling and being picked up — but I am the distance he fell and the hands that lifted him, not the bump in between. I remember the sound of my own voice crying — but not the feel of it. That voice is gone. And I am the gloves my mother wore when she held my hand and the tones of her laughter. And I remember and will move forever, as all children do, to the heartbeats of my mother. That remembrance is the rhythm of my life. So memory is other people — it is little of ourselves.

I like Remembrance Day. I'm fond of memory. I wish it was a day of happiness. I have many dead in my past, but only one of them died from the wars. And I think very fondly of him. He was my uncle. He didn't die in the War, but because of it. This was the First World War and so I don't remember the event itself. I just remember him. But what I remember of my uncle is not the least bit sad.

I was just a child — in the classic sense — a burbling, few-worded, looking-up-at-everything child. Uncle Tif — who died at home — was always in a great tall bed — high up — and the bed was white. I would go into his room, supported by my father's hands, and lean against the lower edge of the mattress. There was a white sheet over everything, and I can smell that sheet to this day. It smelled of soap and talcum powder. To me, Uncle Tif was a hand that came down from a great way off and tapped me on the head. He smoked a pipe. And there was something blue in the room — I don't know whether it was a chair or a table or my father's pant legs — but there was something blue and that has always been one of my favourite colours.

And high above my head, there was a tall glass jar on a table and the jar was full of hard French candies. They had shiny jackets and were many colours. And Uncle Tif's hand would go out, waving in the air above my gaze and lift up the lid of the jar and take out a candy and slowly — it was always slowly — he would pass the candy down into my open mouth. Then I would lean against the bed, or fall on the floor, and taste the candy for about two hours — or what, to a kid, just seemed two hours — while the adult voices buzzed above my head.

I know he sacrificed his youth, his health, his leg and finally his life for his country. But I'd be a fool if I just said *thanks — I'm grateful*. I might as well hit him in the mouth as say that. Because my being grateful has nothing to do with what he died for or why he died. That was part of his own life and what I am grateful for is that he had his own life. I am grateful he was there in that little bit of my life. And I am grateful, above all, that he is in my memory. I am his namesake. He is mine.

Remembrance is more than honouring the dead. Remembrance is joining them — being one with them in memory. Memory is survival.

RESPONSE

1. In your groups, interpret the following statements from Findley's work:
   a) "Memory is making peace with time."
   b) ". . . we are what we remember."
   c) "Remembrance is more than honoring the dead. [It] is joining them."
   d) "Memory is survival."
2. Does your memory of your own childhood work in the same way Findley's does? Explain.

EXTENSION

3. Write an extended remembrance of a person or place known to you.
4. In your group, create a Remembrance Day observance for your school that will be meaningful to your fellow students.

PUTTING ON ARMOR TO FACE THE WORLD

AMY WILLARD CROSS

- Have you ever had a first-hand experience with a burglary or known anyone who has? Explain.
- What thoughts and feelings do you think are associated with the experience?

There's a rock in the middle of my living-room floor. It's been there for several weeks. Somebody chucked it through the window, exploding glass inside and out. They squeezed through a 15-by-15-inch window and made themselves at home. In my house.

The intruders left a silver knife on the kitchen counter, as if considered then rejected. Like my stuff wasn't good enough. All over the house they tossed clumps of matches which had lit their way. In those private drawers of desk and night table, where secrets and valuables hide, their hands groped for cash and jewelry — like the lottery announcer fishing for numbers.

They left each drawer pulled wide open in a defiant Kilroy-was-here gesture — letting all my secrets evaporate into air. Making sure they made a big impression, they scattered my underwear onto the floor. Strangers fishing around in my lingerie wanted me to know about it. That just added a creepy dimension and a couple of question marks to a run-of-the-mill crime.

In the language of cop shows, I had a B & E. It's a verb too, my house was B & E'd. To break and enter is a crime in itself, without adding robbery. Indeed, the maximum penalty is life imprisonment. That I had no cash or jewelry or fancy electronic goods worth stealing doesn't matter. The damages go beyond cash, as anyone who's been robbed, burgled or looted can tell you.

Those thwarted thieves did rob me. They stole my sense of safety. They defrauded me of trust. They took my privacy by trespassing past personal boundaries which mother, roommates and husband had always respected. And I feel ripped off. It's not money; I'd have emptied my wallet to spare the consequences of one broken window and minor fence repair — $50 and change. When you look out at the world through shattered glass, the view suddenly changes.

Despite the proliferation of signs such as "Beware of Dog" and "Protected by Cerberus Alarms," I never imagined I'd get robbed. Robberies happened to people with grand houses, fine things and flashy cars outfitted with stereo systems. When it did, I dialed 911 — the three numbers which promise to remedy the more overwhelming problems in life.

We call the police, although they can't bring back the wallet, car radio, pearls or bike. Like calling doctors when someone dies, the police just confirm it's gone. Surveying the rock and knife I collected as evidence to catch the culprits, the officer said: "Lady, fingerprints are for the movies." So what can they do? They say it happens to everyone, take notes, file a report, and add the casualty to a growing list. Surveying the style of my B & E, the officer pronounced: "Kids, 13-15 looking for cash or jewelry, probably got scared away, before they had a chance to grab anything."

Unfortunately for teens in my neighborhood, each kid playing ball in the park is a potential suspect. Especially the kid who rides a different bike every day. As he described finding and assembling 25 bikes, I calculated whether he'd fit through my window.

Distrust spreads like an itchy rash: My hand reflexively slips into my bag for the reassuring feel of a wallet after being approached by strangers.

After hearing that some B & E professionals occasionally work as roofers to "case out joints," I won't fix a leaky roof. Like other victims of robbery, when objects disappear, I'm convinced they're snitched, rather than fearing I've thrown them absent-mindedly in the garbage like I used to.

My house changed too. No longer my castle, it's a house of cards. I'm reminded of its paper-thick impenetrability whenever I look out of the window, open a drawer, or answer a call that replies "click." My territory was invaded. When returning home after a short errand, my heart beats uncontrollably until I turn the corner and see my window remains intact. I mutter thanks each time.

Like so many others, I started fortifying my castle after the invasion. (I've met only one person who installed an alarm before they had a break-in.) Now there's a bar in my front window to prevent it sliding. Too late. Still I want alarms, timers, bars, anything to assure I never come home to broken glass and ransacked drawers.

Thieves take away more than the objects themselves. After a robbery, the pleasure of ownership — which fuels our hard-working culture — vanishes. It's overpowered by a new-found uneasiness that doesn't go away. Granted, the insurance pays for the replaceable things that carry serial numbers. But even then, after having three car radios stolen, some people can't even bother to fill out more forms; they drive in silence.

Of course, the irreplaceables derive meaning from the people connected to them. They trade in that invisible economy of sentimental value: talismans that don't figure in any actuarial table. For fear of losing it, the silverplate bowl — my best friend's wedding present — was banished into a secure place. My father's old watch, which would hardly be given the time of day in a pawnshop, lives in a safe, too far away to make me lucky on special days like it used to. So in a way these things were indeed taken.

Like traffic accidents or cold sores, getting ripped off is just another initiation in modern life. Sooner or later, it happens to everyone: on a European vacation, in a crowd, or when you've gone for a long weekend with the bathroom light on and the radio playing. But as much as we expect to be ripped off, we can never really get used to it. It just feels too raunchy — like waking up with a tattooed stranger. Some people say having stuff stolen feels violating — like a rape. I wouldn't go that far, but I know it will take time to coax the secrets back into my drawers.

I swept up the glass. I put away the underwear. After a few days, I relinquished all my evidence and trashed the matches. But the rock stays. When it becomes underfoot, I'll move it to a table, where that wedding present once presided. The rock stays to remind me of the precariousness of privacy and the fragility of ownership. But I'd remember anyway.

RESPONSE

1. What do you think Cross means when she writes, "They stole my sense of safety. They defrauded me of trust. They took my privacy . . ."?
2. What do you think of Cross's reaction to the break and enter?

EXTENSION

3. Do you own possessions which have no real value, but which are very important to you? Explain.
4. Ask a police officer to visit your class. Ask the officer about the frequency of breaking and entering in your community and the kinds of sentences that result from conviction of such a crime.

ABOUT MEN

GRETEL EHRLICH

- Characterize the stereotypical cowboy as depicted in the media.
- Do you think this depiction is accurate? Explain.

W hen I'm in New York but feeling lonely for Wyoming I look for the Marlboro ads in the subway. What I'm aching to see is horseflesh, the glint of a spur, a line of distant mountains, brimming creeks, and a reminder of the ranchers and cowboys I've ridden with for the last eight years. But the men I see in those posters with their stern, humorless looks remind me of no one I know here. In our hellbent earnestness to romanticize the cowboy we've ironically disesteemed his true character. If he's "strong and silent" it's because there's probably no one to talk to. If he "rides away into the sunset" it's because he's been on horseback since four in the morning moving cattle and he's trying, fifteen hours later, to get home to his family. If he's "a rugged individualist" he's also part of a team: ranch work is teamwork and even the glorified open-range cowboys of the 1880s rode up and down the Chisholm Trail in the company of twenty or thirty other riders. Instead of the macho, trigger-happy man our culture has perversely wanted him to be, the cowboy is more apt to be convivial, quirky, and softhearted. To be "tough" on a ranch has nothing to do with conquests and displays of power. More often than not, circumstances — like the colt he's riding or an unexpected blizzard — are overpowering him. It's not toughness but "toughing it out" that counts. In other words, this macho, cultural artifact the cowboy has become is simply a man who possesses resilience, patience, and an instinct for survival. "Cowboys are just like a pile of rocks — everything happens to them. They get climbed on, kicked, rained and snowed on, scuffed up by wind. Their job is 'just to take it,' " one old-timer told me.

A cowboy is someone who loves his work. Since the hours are long — ten to fifteen hours a day — and the pay is $30 he has to. What's required of him is an odd mixture of physical vigor and maternalism. His part of the beef-raising industry is to birth and nurture calves and take care of their mothers. For the most part his work is done on horseback and in a lifetime he sees and comes to know more animals than people. The iconic myth surrounding him is built on American notions of heroism: the index of a man's value as measured in physical courage. Such ideas have perverted manliness into a self-absorbed race for cheap thrills. In a rancher's world, courage has less to do with facing danger than with acting spontaneously — usually on behalf of an animal or another rider. If a cow is stuck in a boghole he throws a loop around her neck, takes his dally (a half hitch around the saddle horn), and pulls her out with horsepower. If a calf is born sick, he may take her home, warm her in front of the kitchen fire, and massage her legs until dawn. One friend, whose favorite horse was trying to swim a lake with hobbles on, dove under water and cut her legs loose with a knife, then swam her to shore, his arm around her neck lifeguard-style, and saved her from drowning. Because these incidents are usually linked to someone or something outside himself, the westerner's courage is selfless, a form of compassion.

The physical punishment that goes with cowboying is greatly underplayed. Once fear is dispensed with, the threshold of pain rises to meet the demands of the job. When Jane Fonda asked Robert Redford (in the film *Electric Horseman*) if he was sick as he struggled to his feet one morning, he replied, "No, just bent." For once the movies had it right. The cowboys I was sitting with laughed in agreement. Cowboys are rarely complainers; they show their stoicism by laughing at themselves.

If a rancher or cowboy has been thought of as a "man's man" — laconic, hard-drinking, inscrutable — there's almost no place in which the balancing act between male and female, manliness and femininity, can be more natural. If he's gruff, handsome, and physically fit on the outside, he's androgynous at the core. Ranchers are midwives, hunters, nurturers, providers, and conservationists all at once. What we've interpreted as toughness — weathered skin, calloused hands, a squint in the eye and a growl in the voice — only masks the tenderness inside. "Now don't go telling me these lambs are cute," one rancher warned me the first day I walked into the football-field-sized lambing sheds. The next thing I knew he was holding a black lamb. "Ain't this little rat good-lookin'?"

So many of the men who came to the West were southerners — men looking for work and a new life after the Civil War — that chivalrousness and strict codes of honor were soon thought of as western traits. There were very few women in Wyoming during territorial days, so when they did arrive (some as mail-order brides from places like Philadelphia) there was a stand-offishness between the sexes and a formality that persists now. Ranchers still tip their hats and say, "Howdy, ma'am" instead of shaking hands with me.

Even young cowboys are often evasive with women. It's not that they're Jekyll and Hyde creatures — gentle with animals and rough with women — but rather, that they don't know how to bring their tenderness into the house and lack the vocabulary to express the complexity of what they feel. Dancing wildly all night becomes a metaphor for the explosive emotions pent up inside, and when these are, on occasion, released, they're so battery-charged and potent that one caress of the face or one "I love you" will peal for a long while.

The geographical vastness and the social isolation here make emotional evolution seem impossible. Those contradictions of the heart between respectability, logic, and convention on the one hand, and impulse, passion, and intuition on the other, played out wordlessly against the paradisiacal beauty of the West, give cowboys a wide-eyed but drawn look. Their lips pucker up, not with kisses but with immutability. They may want to break out, staying up all night with a lover just to talk, but they don't know how and can't imagine what the consequences will be. Those rare occasions when they do bare themselves result in confusion. "I feel as if I'd sprained my heart," one friend told me a month after such a meeting.

My friend Ted Hoagland wrote, "No one is as fragile as a woman but no one is as fragile as a man." For all the women here who use "fragileness" to avoid work or as a sexual ploy, there are men who try to hide theirs, all the while clinging to an adolescent dependency on women to cook their meals, wash their clothes, and keep the ranch house warm in winter. But there is true vulnerability in evidence here. Because these men work with animals, not machines or numbers, because they live outside in landscapes of torrential beauty, because they are confined to a place and a routine embellished with awesome variables, because calves die in the arms that pulled others into life, because they go to the mountains as if on pilgrimage to find out what makes a herd of elk tick, their strength is also a softness, their toughness, a rare delicacy.

RESPONSE

1. In groups, select and discuss five statements from the article which are inconsistent with the "iconic myth" of the cowboy.
2. For discussion: "No one is as fragile as a woman but no one is as fragile as a man."

EXTENSION

3. Identify another group of so-called "mythical" persons and then present the reality about that group to your class. You might, for example, consider the following: the stereotypical teacher, the stereotypical farmer, the stereotypical firefighter.
4. "I feel as if I've sprained my heart." Compose a short narrative based on personal experience that dramatizes this quotation.

CHILDREN AND ALCOHOL

JOHN ALLEMANG

- Do you think it is appropriate for adolescents to consume alcohol at home under the supervision of a parent or guardian? Explain.

I am trying to think of something good to say about alcohol. It isn't easy. When everyone knows that alcohol can ruin lives, and sometimes end them, it's hard to argue that drinking is an innocent pleasure. If there is such a thing as an innocent pleasure.

The pleasure was fleeting for a Toronto innocent named Jimmy Whiffen who knocked back five beers and a half bottle of tequila one night last May. He would have had one awful hangover if he'd lived. His decomposing body was found a few days later in a dumpster, where a drinking buddy had tossed it. He was 15. When a coroner's jury came to pass judgment on this sad affair, they had no trouble singling out the villain. "Our overall message," said a jury member, "is that alcohol kills."

Well it can, and it did. But does that make alcohol an evil, as the jury would like us to believe? Health warnings, a ban on advertising, drink-and-drive programs, government control of alcohol — all these things tell me that there is something wrong with me, something morally wrong, every time I choose to drink. And if I'm supposed to feel guilty about taking a drink, what circle of hell do I enter when I give my kids a drink?

I do this once a week on the average. My 9-year-old son claims to like Champagne and a particular brand of beer from Czechoslovakia. My six-year-old daughter enjoys Cabernet Sauvignon wines, although I think what she really enjoys is winding her tongue around the words Cabernet Sauvignon. Sometimes they get a sip or two from my glass, sometimes the dregs of a beer bottle, and if the occasion is special they have their own glass of wine mixed with soda water. I've never seen them show the effects of alcohol, but how do you tell with kids? They seem to take in hallucinogens with the air they breathe.

My reasoning, if the ravings of a steady drinker can be called reasoning, is that my children are learning moderation. By drinking carefully and thoughtfully under the watchful eye of their parents, they won't see alcohol as a form of rebellion or a useful shortcut to unconsciousness.

Those are high-sounding words, but I can't convince myself that they're entirely true. I don't offer my children cigarettes or hashish or cocaine to teach them moderation. Why should alcohol be any different? Yes, it's legal after a certain age, and less likely to hurt them than tobacco. But still I know that at some point in the next few years they're going to make a habit of drinking themselves silly. I did, at the same age as the late Jimmy Whiffen and in much the same quantity.

It's the Canadian Way.

So at the same time that I pretend with my children that wine and beer aren't deadly drugs, I try to get them to think about the damage that booze can do. When we see a drunk weaving down the street or a couple of lite-beer addicts cavorting at the old ballpark, I switch into my moralizing mode. "That guy's had too much to drink," I'll say, and hope, for their father's sake, that they can grasp the difference between enough and too much. When an awful beer commercial comes on, and some dumb hunk is putting the moves on the one woman in 1,000 who weighs 110 pounds and has a 38-inch chest, I make gagging sounds.

"What does this have to do with beer?" I cry out. My son is so well trained that he now says it before I do.

But of course it has a lot to do with beer. If beer were only about the chemical reaction of barley and water, who would drink it? Except when it kills, alcohol is about lifestyles, and the one I'm teaching my kids is just one of many. Alcohol is a way of pretending that you're different from who you are. The lugs who believe the beer ads, the Cabernet drinkers who get soused at dinner parties, and the mother who likes the distancing effect of a Campari-and-soda at the end of a long day, all of them want to escape, perhaps even need to escape.

Hypocrisy doesn't kill, very often, but I think it's more dangerous to kids than alcohol. I don't want my kids to see me drunk, because it's hard enough to command respect sober, but I don't like to hear my voice taking on the moral certainty of our neotemperance culture. Alcohol can help us reflect, relax, make believe. There are worse things.

RESPONSE

1. Do you think that Allemang's motives for allowing his children to drink at home are justifiable? Explain.
2. For discussion: "Alcohol is a way of pretending you are different from who you are."
3. Allemang claims that the habit of drinking oneself silly at fifteen is "the Canadian Way." Do you think this view is justified?

EXTENSION

4. Account for the high incidence of alcohol abuse among adolescents.
5. Contact the authorities in your community to research the relationship between alcohol abuse and such social problems as impaired driving and family violence.

KELLY AND CONNIE

MYRNA KOSTASH

- In groups, speculate on why there aren't more professional women's teams and why there are fewer well-known female than male professional athletes.
- Which are the most popular teams in your school from the spectators' point of view?
- When was the last time your school was dismissed early for a girls' sporting event?

W earing the number six sweater (a dark-blue shirt with a white collar), with grey shorts and blue knee-pads, Kelly is warming up for this afternoon's game against the Salisbury Sabres. She's in grade eleven at Ross Sheppard, a classic "all-rounded" student who does well in chemistry and French, plays the clarinet in the school band, works on weekends at a boutique in a shopping mall, and plays on the school's junior girls' Thunderbirds volleyball team. She loves sports best of all.

The junior girls play in the small gym (the boys' teams work out in the large one), and so, because there are no bleachers, those of us who've come to watch the game — a handful of girls, a sprinkling of teachers, one or two boyfriends — sit on the floor,

---

slouching against the wall. This is an important game: if the Shep girls lose it, they're out for the season. Still, no one is particularly keyed-up. The Salisbury team (from a lower-middle-class suburb) arrives, looking somehow meaner (bulkier, grimmer) than the Shep girls. As it does its warm-up stretches, a Shep player drives a sudden spike ball into the midst of them. It is the first challenge the Shep girls will offer Salisbury.

Sadly, it is also the last. Shep plays badly. Balls hit the ceiling, are fired at the players' bench, and fall inconsequentially wide of the court. For all that, the players exhibit a lot of energy and enthusiasm, accompanying their lacklustre performance with much jumping up and down and a great deal of hand-clapping and shrieking. Whenever a Shep server scores a point, the rest of her team rush around her, giddily congratulating her and reaching out their hands to touch her as though she were a talisman of luck. But it is in vain. In spite of the occasional plucky yelp — "Go, T-Birds!" — and Kelly's own swift, clean serves across the net, ten minutes into the third game they are trailing 8 to 1 and are visibly wilting. They trip over their feet and fall over each other. "That's girls' sports for you — hysteria," grumbles a male coach who's wandered in from the other gym to watch. "They're more concerned about how they look than with saving the ball." With all due respect to his professional's eye, I don't think that is the problem here: in their efforts to keep the ball in play they dive and slide along the floor, without effect. They lose.

Kelly will explain to me later that the T-Birds lost to the Sabres not because their opponents were much superior but because "when we started to get beaten some people thought, 'Why even try?' Once you start losing, it's really hard to get yourself back up." "Why even try" is a long way from the sort of distilled blood-lust one associates with the (male) athlete, and with the ardent labour of the body exerting itself at all costs to win. Why should women's games be so different? The shallow observation that young women are anxious about their appearance is hardly an explanation. What is at issue here is their relationship to their *body*: even to the inexpert eye, most teenage girls seem to inhabit it somewhat gingerly, as though to wield it forcefully would be to damage or hurt it.

At this game and elsewhere — in physical education classes, at games of badminton and volleyball — I watch fifteen- and sixteen-year-olds move with minimal exertion, as though their bodies were already ponderous and somehow disabled. It is interesting that a 1986 McMaster University study found that among fourteen- to sixteen-year-olds in Ontario more girls than boys smoke tobacco, drink alcohol, and sniff inhalants such as glue and gasoline. A recent Participaction report that teenage girls are the least fit people in Canada raises the question whether this lack of fitness is the cause of the sluggishness or its consequence. Is it possible that girls avoid fitness in some misguided pursuit of feminine tenderness? Alongside the occasional images in magazines and on television of young women in neon-bright outfits lifting weights in post-modern spa interiors, a much older, much more deeply rooted image competes for the identity of girls: the woman at leisure, languid upon her chaise longue, gazing into a mirror, absorbed in the passivity of her own useless flesh, her body awaiting the quickening touch of a lover. *This* is femininity. To be lithe and quick, rambunctious and on the move, is to be a kid, a sexless kid. Kids run around whacking balls. *Women* lean back, striking poses.

Kelly, though, is not like this. Her coach calls her a "fine athlete": she has a strong body, good hand and eye co-ordination, and an acute sense of timing. "She's receptive, is able to translate an instruction immediately through her body." She's weakest as a sprinter, strongest as a long-distance runner and in the water. It's a question now of maturing into a disciplined *artist* whose body performs no more, and no less, than what it is instructed to do. Kelly doubts that she will get to that point: she sees herself as a competent athlete, good at many sports — soccer, track, volleyball — but not outstanding at any particular game. She accepts this. She plays for the love of it.

This, more than any other reason, is probably why Kelly will never be a star athlete. For it is not love but aggressive, single-minded competitiveness that wins games, and while Kelly will try her hardest, she feels that "it's not the worst thing in the world to lose." She finds it hard to train for track, for instance; rather than submit to the grinding routine of training, she prefers to get out and *run*, flying into the wind. It doesn't even have to be a race. It isn't personal glory she's after: for her, one of the keenest satisfactions of sport is to play with a team, to connect and share with others, and, of course, once you have the sense of connection with fellow players it becomes impossible *not* to worry what you're prepared to do to win. "Usually we won't ever show feelings of anger towards each other during a game. You just can't let that happen. Everyone is going to make a few mistakes and that's to be expected. Like in a soccer game, you're playing for an hour and a half and nobody thinks that every time you approach the ball you're going to do something perfect with it." It feels good to win, she won't deny it, but that isn't half the pleasure of the great, gulping relief to be *finished* a race, a game. To have done it, period.

But girl athletes pay a penalty for their femininity. According to a report in the *Globe and Mail* ("Girls Winning the Sports War Against Shutouts"), male-run sports organizations do not promote female athletes, pay them very little, and seem to hope that from sheer inattention they'll go away. To give one example, the Ontario Lacrosse Association spends a total of $160,000, of which its women's team receives $5,000. The Supreme Court of Ontario has ruled that girls may not play with boys in the minor hockey leagues, but a twelve-year-old girl has initiated a discrimination complaint with the Ontario Human Rights Commission all the same. Her persistence is remarkable; by the time they reach high school, most girls have become sufficiently discouraged by the hostility of the male-dominated athletic milieu, and by the visible impoverishment of the female sector, not to mention the innuendoes regarding female jocks, that they avoid physical assertiveness wherever they can, taking physical education classes only if they have to, and dragging their laggard bodies along with them. It is not, to put it mildly, the stuff of which champion volleyball teams are built.

Kelly acknowledges all of this: that girl teams don't have fans, that even the most sports-minded boy will rarely make a point of watching a girls' game, that the interest is so tepid because the girls' "skill level" is so much lower; if the senior girls' basketball team, for instance, were to play the senior boys', they'd be slaughtered. She understands why it would seem to a male athlete that girl athletes are not *serious*: she remembers in phys ed class how many girls objected to the instruction to *squat down* to be ready for the ball; they said they felt "stupid" in that position, especially if a boy were watching: "ladies" don't squat. But she rejects the notion that any female player she knows would "let a ball drop on the floor just to look good. Everyone else would wonder how you got on the team."

No, the difference goes much deeper than that: girls simply aren't as competitive as boys. All his life, Kelly argues, a boy has been told he can get somewhere in sports: win an athletic scholarship, be a big hero. But girls do not have this incentive, for the simple reason that girls' sports do not "go" anywhere. Where is professional women's basketball, soccer, hockey? Towards which goal, exactly, is a woman athlete called on to compete? Unsurprisingly, girls have different *feelings* from boys when they play. "Boys withdraw into themselves when they're upset in games," Kelly has observed. "They become very moody, but girls will yell and scream and try to boost each other up. When guys lose, they blame it on themselves and it's the end of the world. When we girls lose, we say, 'Oh well, there's always tomorrow's game, it's no big deal. We all did the best we could. What else could be done?' "

It's a matter of some debate whether these feelings are "natural" to women and to female culture, and ought, in fact, to be encouraged in the name of co-operativeness and tolerance and uncorrupted playfulness. The other possibility is that they reflect physical timorousness and a certain feminine lack of gumption, as though to be very strong and very talented were to invite some kind of punishment. "Sometimes," says Kelly, "I think a girl is afraid of doing too well. You kind of want to be average, you don't want to stand out."

But Kelly is not losing any sleep over it. What *she* knows is that she's got muscled legs but weak forearms, that she's terrible at baseball but pretty good at hurdles, that she looks good — she's not just skin and bones — and feels good and loves to horse around with her team-mates and call some of them her friends, all of it the gift of her enthusiasm.

It is a conceit of adults raised before the installation of a television set in every Canadian home that no young person since that watershed event has known how to amuse herself. The function of the imagination, so the argument goes, once an idiosyncratic instrument harboured in the memory and dreams of the person, has now been transferred to the solid-state mechanisms of the "box," relieving us all of the obligation to generate our own pleasures. Of whom could this be more true than the current generation of teenagers, who have been relieved not only of this onerous task, but of countless others? They are no longer obliged to read, for instance, learning speech and the collective wisdom of their culture from *conversation* and the electronic media; they need not write but only *tell* us what's on their mind; the skill of banging out popular tunes on the piano has been made redundant by the one-button marvels of the synthesizer. Meanwhile, the convivial group around the radio has shrivelled to an audience of one, her Walkman plugs in her ears, absorbed in the very private pleasure of a song shared with no one. Given the pervasiveness of all these modes of entertainment, and the passivity with which they are consumed, it has been assumed of post-sixties young people that they are creatures in whom imagination (and, therefore, self-generated pleasure) lies desiccated and puny, like a vestigial digit.

This may very well be true at the level of some broad and scientific sociometric investigation, but it is certainly not true at the level of the individual and anecdotal experience: Kelly practises swinging her arm like a pendulum so that the arc of its sweep will send the volleyball in flight just so, and Connie lifts weights because a strong arm and shoulder is a beautiful thing that works as it was meant to, and Nina, whom we will meet later, stretches out in splits in the air because she imagines herself a free being inhabiting space where before there was only vacancy. The wonder of it all is that, in spite of the tyrannical presence of the entertainment media and their capacity to fill in every leftover space with sound and fury, in spite of the unchallenged assumptions of mass culture that no one should be left for a moment alone with her own thoughts, and in spite of the terrific pressures from teen society that bear down and flatten individual peculiarities (oddities of manner, speech, aspiration), these girls have managed to appropriate some activity, name it, and imprint it with their own fantasy.

To pursue *her* enthusiasm, Connie had to invade a male sanctuary, the weight-training room in the basement of her school. She had never thought of herself as someone who would want to lift fifty pounds with one arm, but when she heard over the school intercom that a weight-training instructor was available, she nudged a couple of girlfriends and said, let's go for it. She'll admit now that there was an element of "faddishness" in what they wanted to do and something "intriguing" about their pioneering effort — three girls in a roomful of guys pumping iron who curled their lips and snorted at their arrival. She was at first repelled by the fetid and grimy atmosphere in the small room: "When there's a bunch of guys in there it really stinks, you can almost smell the dampness on their bodies. It's gross, like a guys' locker-room." But as more girls arrived to train, the air improved considerably (deodorant, baby powder, "Charlie" cologne), and the body-builders, accepting the new status quo, went back to their single-minded concentration on the bench press and the barbells. Eventually, Connie found her own reasons to be there after the excitement of shocking male peers had worn off. As she puts it, "I'm not doing it just to be cool."

"It," however, is not the awesome effort of the young men at the chin-bars and the leg presses, rhythmically repeating the exercise with a glazed look on their faces as though hypnotized by the staggering monotony of their labours, or the boy lifting fifty pounds, just like that, from floor to chest, over and over and over again, the slabs of his muscles appearing and disappearing beneath his skin in a weird choreography of the flesh. What Connie is doing is more leisurely: a few bench-press repetitions and a brief workout with the hamstring curls and the thigh extenders (ten pounds), with pauses in between during which she drapes herself over the equipment, and chats with a friend who is flexing her arm and proudly displaying a bulge of bicep. The instructor, herself a competitive body-builder who trains three hours every day, says there's "no difference" between the training men and women do on this equipment, and that Connie (who doesn't "think she can do anything more") could be working a lot harder.

But it is obviously not Connie's ambition to be a body-builder, to become (in the eye of some beholders) a grotesque caricature of the male physique: she is here to improve her "body tone," to keep the fat off, to banish the softness and mushiness (as she perceives them) of her too-feminine body, which still, to her disgust, cannot move very heavy objects, obliging her to call upon the aid of a male. What she *enjoys* about this workout, it seems to me, is the revelation of the stamina and accumulating power and comeliness of her very own body — not of some idealized Wonder

Woman, challenging the muscular pre-eminence of men in their own shape. There she lies — long and slender legs astride a bench, her boyish buttocks pressed down against it, and the spheres of her breasts wrapped under the T-shirt which is riding up her flat and narrow midriff — triumphantly pushing twenty pounds of lead.

RESPONSE

1. Discuss with your group your thoughts and feelings about the following statements: "Teenage girls are the least fit people in Canada."
2. Assess Kelly's attitude towards athletics and her participation in sport.
3. "Girl athletes pay a penalty for their femininity." How is this statement borne out in your school and community?
4. In your group, discuss Connie's attitude towards weight training.

EXTENSION

5. In the resource centre, compile a short report on a Canadian female athlete. Present your findings to the class.
6. As a group, compile a report on sport in your school. You may wish to consider the following factors:
   a) the number of teams — male and female
   b) the number of team members — male and female
   c) the number of students enrolled in physical education classes — male and female
   d) the amount of money spent on male and female teams
   e) other factors which you think should be taken into consideration.
   You may wish to make recommendations to the appropriate school authorities.

OUR DAUGHTERS, OURSELVES

STEVIE CAMERON

* Do you think life is harder for girls than it is for boys? Explain.

They are so precious to us, our daughters. When they are born we see their futures as unlimited, and as they grow and learn we try so hard to protect them: This is how we cross the street, hold my hand, wear your boots, don't talk to strangers, run to the neighbors if a man tries to get you in his car.

We tell our bright, shining girls that they can be anything: firefighters, doctors, policewomen, lawyers, scientists, soldiers, athletes, artists. What we don't tell them, yet, is how hard it will be. Maybe, we say to ourselves, by the time they're older it will be easier for them than it was for us.

But as they grow and learn, with aching hearts we have to start dealing with their bewilderment about injustice. Why do the boys get the best gyms, the best equipment and the best times on the field? Most of the school sports budget? Why does football matter more than gymnastics? Why are most of the teachers women and most of the principals men? Why do the boys make more money at their part-time jobs than we do?

And as they grow and learn we have to go on trying to protect them: We'll pick you up at the subway, we'll fetch you from the movie, stay with the group, make sure the parents drive you home from babysitting, don't walk across the park alone, lock the house if we're not there.

It's not fair, they say. Boys can walk where they want, come in when they want, work where they want. Not really, we say: boys get attacked too. But boys are not targets for men the way girls are, so girls have to be more careful.

Sometimes our girls don't make it. Sometimes, despite our best efforts and all our love, they go on drugs, drop out, screw up. On the whole, however, our daughters turn into interesting, delightful people. They plan for college and university, and with wonder and pride we see them competing with the boys for spaces in engineering schools, medical schools, law schools, business schools. For them we dream of Rhodes scholarships, Harvard graduate school, gold medals: sometimes, we even dare to say these words out loud and our daughters reward us with indulgent hugs. Our message is that anything is possible.

We bite back the cautions that we feel we should give them: maybe by the time they've graduated, things will have changed, we say to ourselves. Probably by the time they're out, they will make partner when the men do, be asked to join the same clubs, run for political office. Perhaps they'll even be able to tee off at the same time men do at the golf club.

But we still warn them: park close to the movie, get a deadbolt for your apartment, check your windows, tell your roommates where you are. Call me. Call me.

And then with aching hearts we take our precious daughters to lunch and listen to them talk about their friends: the one who was beaten by her boy friend and then shunned by his friends when she asked for help from the dean; the one who was attacked in the parking lot; the one who gets obscene and threatening calls from a boy in her residence; the one who gets raped on a date; the one who was mocked by the male students in the public meeting.

They tell us about the sexism they're discovering in the adult world at university. Women professors who can't get jobs, who can't get tenure. Male professors who cannot comprehend women's stony silence after sexist jokes. An administration that only pays lip service to women's issues and refuses to accept the reality of physical danger to women on campus.

They tell us they're talking among themselves about how men are demanding rights over unborn children, it's not old dinosaurs who go to court to prevent a woman's abortion, it's young men. It's young men, they say with disbelief, their own generation, their own buddies with good education, from "nice" families, who are abusive.

What can we say to our bright and shining daughters? How can we tell them how much we hurt to see them developing the same scars we've carried? How much we wanted it to be different for them? It's all about power, we say to them. Sharing power is not easy for anyone and men do not find it easy to share among themselves, much less with a group of equally talented, able women. So men make all those stupid cracks about needing a sex-change operation to get a job or a promotion and they wind up believing it.

Now our daughters have been shocked to the core, as we all have, by the violence in Montreal. They hear the women were separated from the men and meticulously slaughtered by a man who blamed feminists for his troubles. They ask themselves why nobody was able to help the terrified women, to somehow stop the hunter as he roamed the engineering building.

So now our daughters are truly frightened and it makes their mothers furious that they are frightened. They survived all the childhood dangers, they were careful as we trained them to be, they worked hard. Anything was possible and our daughters proved it. And now they are more scared than they were when they were little girls.

Fourteen of our bright and shining daughters won places in engineering schools, doing things we, their mothers, only dreamed of. That we lost them has broken our hearts; what is worse is that we are not surprised.

RESPONSE

1. Answer each question that Cameron poses in the third paragraph of her essay.
2. Cameron claims that sexism "is all about power," and "sharing power is not easy for anyone." In your group, assess the validity of this statement.

EXTENSION

3. In your group, develop a questionnaire concerning conditions for female students in your school in terms of security, welfare, and equality of opportunity. Administer the questionnaire, compile the data, and present your findings to your student council.

FISH, FLESH, AND FOWL

KNOW THAT WHAT YOU EAT YOU ARE

WENDELL BERRY

- Where does most of the food you consume come from?
For discussion in your groups:
- How much time in a day do you spend eating?
- Describe the context of those meals. For example: Where do you eat? With whom? Is there conversation? Etc.

M any times, after I have finished a lecture on the decline of American farming and rural life, someone in the audience has asked, "What can city people do?"

"Eat responsibly," I have usually answered. Of course. I have tried to explain what I meant, but afterward I have invariably felt that there was more to be said than I had been able to say. Now I would like to attempt a better explanation.

I begin with the proposition that eating is an agricultural act. Eating ends the annual drama of the food economy that begins with planting and birth. Most eaters, however, are no longer aware that this is true. They think of food as an agricultural product perhaps, but they do not think of themselves as participants in agriculture. They think of themselves as "consumers."

Most urban shoppers would tell you that food is produced on farms. But most of them do not know on what farms, or what kinds of farms, or where the farms are, or what knowledge and skills are involved in farming. For them, then, food is pretty much an abstract idea — something they do not know or imagine — until it appears on the grocery shelf or on the table. Indeed, this sort of consumption may be said to be one of the chief goals of industrial production. The food industrialists have by now persuaded millions of consumers to prefer food that is already prepared. They will grow, deliver, and cook your food for you, and (just like your mother) beg you to eat it. That they do not yet offer to insert it, prechewed, into your mouth is only because they have found no profitable way to do so.

The industrial eater is one who no longer knows that eating is an agricultural act, who no longer knows or imagines the connections between eating and the land, and who is therefore necessarily passive and uncritical — in short, a victim. When food, in the minds of eaters, is no longer associated with farming and with the land, then the eaters are suffering from a kind of cultural amnesia that is misleading and dangerous.

There is a politics of food that, like any politics, involves our freedom. We still (sometimes) remember that we cannot be free if our minds and voices are controlled by someone else. But we have neglected to understand that neither can we be free if our food and its sources are controlled by someone else. The condition of the passive consumer of food is not a democratic condition. One reason to eat responsibly is to live free.

But if there is a food politics, there are also a food aesthetics and a food ethics, neither of which is dissociated from politics. The passive American consumer, sitting down to a meal of preprepared or fast food, confronts a platter covered with inert, anonymous substances that have been processed, dyed, breaded, sauced, gravied, ground, pulped, strained, blended, prettified, and sanitized beyond resemblance to any part of any creature that ever lived. The products of nature and agriculture have been made, to all appearances, the products of industry. Both eater and eaten are thus in exile from biological reality. And the result is a kind of solitude, unprecedented in human experience, in which the eater may think of eating as, first, a purely commercial transaction between him and a supplier, and then as a purely appetitive transaction between him and his food.

This peculiar specialization of the act of eating is of obvious benefit to the food industry, which has good reason to obscure the connection between food and farming. It would not do for the consumer to know that the hamburger she is eating came from a steer that spent much of its life standing deep in its own excrement in a feedlot, helping to pollute the local streams, or that the calf that yielded the veal cutlet on her plate spent its life in a box in which it did not have enough room to turn around. And though her sympathy for the coleslaw might be less tender, she should not be encouraged to meditate on the hygienic and biological implications of mile-square fields of cabbage, for vegetables grown in huge monocultures are dependent on toxic chemicals just as animals in close confinement are dependent on antibiotics and other drugs.

The consumer, that is to say, must be kept from discovering that in the food industry — as in any other industry — the overriding concerns are not quality and health but volume and price. For decades now the entire industrial food economy has relentlessly increased scale in order to increase volume in order (presumably) to reduce costs. But as scale increases, diversity declines; as diversity declines, so does health; as health declines, the dependence on drugs and chemicals necessarily increases. Machines, drugs, and chemicals are substituted for human workers and for the natural health and fertility of the soil. The food is produced by any means or any shortcuts that will increase profits. And the business of the cosmeticians of advertising persuades the consumer that food so produced is good, tasty, healthful, and a guarantee of marital fidelity and long life.

How does one escape this trap? Only voluntarily, the same way that one went in — by restoring one's consciousness of what is involved in eating, by reclaiming responsibility for one's own part in the food economy. Eaters, that is, must understand that eating takes place inescapably in the world, that it is inescapably an agricultural act, and that how we eat determines, to a considerable extent, the way the world is used.

What can one do? Here is a list, probably not definitive:

- Participate in food production to the extent that you can. If you have a yard or even just a porch box or a pot in a sunny window, grow something to eat in it. Make a little compost of your kitchen scraps, and become acquainted with the energy cycle that revolves from soil to seed to flower to fruit to food to offal to decay, and around again. You will be fully responsible for any food that you grow for yourself, and you will know all about it. You will appreciate it fully, having known it all its life.
- Prepare your own food. This means reviving in your own mind and life the arts of kitchen and household. This should both enable you to eat more cheaply and, since you will have some reliable knowledge of what has been added to the food you eat, give you a measure of "quality control."
- Learn the origins of the food you buy, and buy the food that is produced closest to your home. The idea that every locality should be, as much as possible, the source of its own food makes several kinds of sense. The locally produced food supply is the most secure, the freshest, and the easiest for local consumers to know about and to influence.
- Whenever you can, deal directly with a local farmer, gardener, or orchardist. By such dealing you eliminate the whole pack of merchants, transporters, processors, packagers, and advertisers who thrive at the expense of both producers and consumers.
- Learn, in self-defense, as much as you can about the economy and technology of industrial food production. What is added to food that is not food, and what do you pay for these additions?
- Learn what is involved in the *best* farming and gardening.
- Learn as much as you can, by direct observation and experience if possible, of the life histories of the animals and plants that you eat.

The last suggestion seems particularly important to me. Many people are now as much estranged from the lives of domestic plants and animals (except for flowers and dogs and cats) as they are from the lives of the wild ones. This is regrettable, for these domestic creatures are in diverse ways attractive; there is much pleasure in knowing them. And at their best, farming, horticulture, animal husbandry, and gardening are complex and comely arts; there is much pleasure in knowing them too.

And it follows that there is great displeasure in knowing about a food economy that degrades and abuses those arts and those plants and animals and the soil from which they come. Though I am by no means a vegetarian, I dislike the thought that some animal has been made miserable in order to feed me. If I am going to eat meat, I want it to be from an animal that has lived a pleasant, uncrowded life outdoors, on bountiful pasture, with good water nearby and trees for shade. And I am getting almost as fussy about food plants. I like to eat vegetables and fruits that have lived happily and healthily in good soil — not the products of the huge, be-chemicaled factory-fields that I have seen, for example, in the Central Valley of California. The industrial farm is said to have been patterned on the factory production line. In practice, it invariably looks more like a concentration camp than a farm.

The pleasure of eating should be an extensive pleasure, not that of the mere gourmet. A significant part of the pleasure of eating is in one's accurate consciousness of the lives and the world from which food comes. And this pleasure, I think, is pretty fully available to the urban consumer who will make the necessary effort.

I mentioned earlier the politics, aesthetics, and ethics of food. But to speak of the pleasure of eating is to go beyond those categories. Eating with the fullest pleasure — pleasure, that is, that does not depend on ignorance — is perhaps the profoundest enactment of our connection with the world. In this pleasure we experience and celebrate our dependence and our gratitude, for we are living from creatures we did not make and powers we cannot comprehend; we are living from mystery. When I think of the meaning of food, I always remember these lines by the poet William Carlos Williams, which seem to me merely honest:

There is nothing to eat,
   seek it where you will,
      but the body of the Lord.
The blessed plants
   and the sea, yield it
      to the imagination
intact.

RESPONSE

1. ". . . how we eat determines . . . the way the world is used." Discuss the validity of this statement in terms of your own experience.
2. Evaluate the practicality of Berry's list of suggestions. In your group devise suggestions of your own.
3. Do you think that Berry is overstating the case when he writes, ". . . we are living from creatures we did not make and powers we cannot comprehend; we are living from mystery"?

EXTENSION

4. Talk to the manager of your local grocery store. Ask him/her about the origin and transportation of the produce s/he sells.
5. Interview the butcher in your local supermarket about the nature of his/her work and products.
6. In the resource centre, research what is involved in "organic gardening" and present your findings to the class.

HAMBURGER HEAVEN

RUSS McNEIL

- How many hamburgers do you eat in the course of a year? How many pounds of ground beef does that number represent? What percentage of your body weight does that number represent?
- How many hamburgers do you think can be derived from one steer?

A hamburger seems such a simple thing. Some advertisers go as far as calling it a "beautiful thing." It is the stock in trade of a dozen multinational fast food outlets which have parlayed our North American obsession with the hamburger into multi-billion dollar industries. The commercial saturation of the hamburger is so pervasive that "McDonald's" is among the first words used by children — long before they have even seen a real hamburger — let alone eaten one. Fast food marketers are very clever people.

I'd be a hypocrite to knock the hamburger. When I was in high school in the '60s, truly good hamburgers were as scarce as hen's teeth. Every Saturday, after the sock hop, a group of us actually took to driving 20 miles out of the city to buy what was a rarity then, a flame-broiled hamburger. These were and still are the messiest things you could imagine — impossible to eat in a car with any degree of decorum — yet, we tried.

The difficulty with hamburgers has nothing to do with nutrition, or health, or calories. The problem with hamburgers is we may be eating too many — more, that is, than our planet can safely produce. It goes like this. In order to satisfy our enormous demand for hamburgers, especially cheap hamburgers, fast food outlets, particularly those in the United States, have to import enormous quantities of lower-cost lean beef from other countries. Much of these imports comes from Central America. There is nothing really wrong with this. Except that in order to produce this beef, Central American countries have had to convert equally enormous tracts of tropical forest into cattle pasture. And it's here where our dilemma occurs. Two U.S. biologists who are very concerned about the loss of these forests, which they call the world's "last bastion of biological diversity," have done some extraordinary calculations to make their point.

The scientists, writing in the journal, *Bioscience*, show that each single average 100-gram hamburger (about 4 ounces) made from beef produced in Central America for North American consumption, represents a loss of tropical forest roughly equal to the area of a small kitchen, about 5 square metres.

They arrived at this figure by showing that cattle on average gain about 23 kilograms a year and need about 0.4 hectares of pasture to do this. During the eight years cattle graze before slaughter, they will gain 182 kilograms, only half of which is useful as food — about 800 hamburgers. They go on to argue that had this "one-hamburger" land area not been converted to pasture it would have supported nearly one-half ton of tropical plants and animals including one large tree, 50 saplings, several thousand insects, animals and birds and a variety of mosses, fungi and other tiny life forms.

It is sobering to contemplate this ecological consequence of eating one imported hamburger, but it is a contemplation we might all begin to consider before our conditioned habits help destroy what remains of one of the remaining wonders of the natural world.

RESPONSE

1. What is the writer's objection to North Americans' consumption of hamburgers? Do you think that his objection is valid? Explain.

2. Do you find McNeil's explanation of the "consequence of eating one imported hamburger" convincing? Explain.

EXTENSION

3. What are some of the ecological consequences of "fast food"?
4. What can you do in your school about these consequences?

A GIFTED TEACHER IN JAPAN

DAVID SUZUKI

- In groups, recount something you learned from one of your
  elementary school teachers. Why has this lesson stayed with
  you?

The Japanese word *sensei* means *teacher* and implies a
great deal of respect, because teaching is such an
honoured profession in Japan. In March 1987, I attended a meeting in Yokohama, where I met a remark-
able *sensei*, Toshiko Toriyama. She is a lone voice fighting against
a rigid educational system that she says is taking a terrible toll
among Japan's children.

Children are put under incredible pressure to perform, beginning in kindergarten and continuing right through high school.
That's because their future opportunities depend so much on
which university accepts them. Toriyama told me the system is so
rigid that by the third week in grade 1 a child must have reached a
specified page in the textbook. Toriyama has rebelled against this
system and tried a radically different approach that has got her
into a lot of trouble with the educational authorities. They have
tried to transfer her to teach the upper years in primary school,

where the children are less impressionable. She has fought to stay with grades 1 to 3, where she believes she has the greatest effect. She may have been turfed out by now.

Japanese school schedules are very rigid; classes begin on the hour, and each subject is taught for fifty minutes. Toriyama designed a flexible schedule, letting the children pursue a topic for two hours or more, depending on their interest and concentration. Toriyama was galvanized into action when she realized that her students, who live in the heart of Tokyo, had never touched a live animal and often did not realize that neatly packaged food in stores was once living organisms.

At the meeting in Yokohama, she demonstrated her teaching techniques before about 500 people. She began by asking questions such as, "Were you alive before you were born?" Then she would answer that each of us lived inside our mother's body for about 270 days, starting from a fertilized egg. "What other animals begin their lives as eggs?" she asked. Gradually we realized that *all* other animals start out the same way. She then took us through growing up and getting old and dying. "All people die; it is nature's way," she told us.

Toriyama then went on to show us the life of a swallowtail butterfly from the time the eggs are laid on a pepper leaf, through hatching, moulting, and pupation. She showed pictures of newly emerged butterflies and of butterfly predators such as spiders and rodents. Then she showed how the butterflies mate, lay eggs, and die. She did the same for praying mantises and coral organisms. She had us close our eyes and imagine we were insects and soon we were wriggling to get out of our skins and dodging animals trying to eat us. It was a brilliant way to show our similarity to other organisms — to demonstrate our relatedness with other life forms.

Toriyama then described an electrifying experiment. She took a grade 3 class on a trip to the country, something almost unheard of in Japan. Once there, she told the city kids to go off and play on their own. In a couple of hours, they began to straggle back, tired and hungry. As they all gathered round asking to be fed, she produced a live chicken. They were fascinated with it as she showed its feathers, claws, and so on. Then she announced, "This is your meal." The children were horrified. Some cried and others begged her not to hurt the chicken. So they had a talk about food, and for the first time they realized that the cooked meat they ate had once been a living animal.

Eventually, hunger overcame their reluctance and the children agreed to eat the chicken. Toriyama helped them kill the bird, pluck it, clean it, and eventually cut it up and cook it. It was a profound lesson, but the school authorities were furious with her. However, the parents were astounded to see a remarkable change in their children's attitude as a result of that experience — they were deeply aware that they depended on living things for their own nourishment.

Toriyama took a live pig to class, again educating the children about the animal. Then she took them to a slaughterhouse where pigs are slaughtered and she had the children hold parts of the viscera — the heart, lungs and stomach.

"What food do we eat that did not come from a living organism?" she asked us. I was amazed to reflect on it and could only come up with two things — salt and water.

Toriyama's radical approach is much more than a way to educate children about the facts of life. It is an attempt to reconnect these children to their biological roots. To her, nourishment, sexuality, and death are natural, to be accepted and appreciated. I'm sure her students will come out as very different adults from graduates of conventional classes. Toshiko Toriyama is a tiny voice amidst the cacophony of high-tech barkers. She will not last long in a society determined to prepare children for the computerized world of the twenty-first century.

RESPONSE

1. Why do you think the school authorities were furious with Toriyama?
2. What evidence is there that Toriyama's students responded in the way she wished?
3. Do you think that Suzuki is correct when he asserts that Toriyama "will not last long in a society determined to prepare children for the computerized world of the twenty-first century"?

EXTENSION

4. Imagine you are Toriyama. Write a letter to the educational authorities explaining why you do what you do.
5. Imagine you were a student on Toriyama's field trip. Write a journal entry about the day's experiences.

RAW SEAL AND THE SPIRIT OF PLENTY

JILL OAKES

- As a class, list the different kinds of food you have eaten which are usually associated with a specific nationality or ethnic group.
- What animals, fruits, and vegetables which are commonly eaten are indigenous to Canada?

W alking along the rocky, ice strewn shore of Arctic Bay, I wondered how I could cope with the exorbitant cost of food. Apples and oranges were $1.50 each, five pounds of potatoes cost $15.00 and a head of lettuce was $9.95. I was conducting field research on skin footwear for my Masters of Science (Human Ecology) degree and had a scant operating budget.

On the beach I met a hunter who guided me to a seal carcass and suggested that I help myself whenever I was hungry. I eagerly boiled up a portion of the rich, dark reddish-black seal meat and ate it for breakfast, lunch, and supper. Seal meat is a good source of protein, iron, B vitamins, and vitamin A. It is also a good source of vitamin C when eaten raw and contains some calcium.

Several days later, a large group of people gathered on the beach close to "my" seal carcass. A hunter's nine-year-old grandson had caught his first seal and everyone was invited to share in the feast. Elizapea Alooloo, a highly respected elder, motioned me to squeeze in next to her. Elizapea gave me my first intimate lesson on how to get a well-balanced diet by following traditional Inuit eating habits. Since then, many Inuit from all regions of the Canadian Arctic have taught me the value of land foods.

Elizapea's first choice of cuts was the intestine. I followed her like a shadow as she carefully disengaged the intestines from the rest of the internal parts and set them aside on the rocks. She selected a section of the small intestine and offered it to me. We ate the thin, outer layer raw.

Since then, on winter camping trips, Inuit have served frozen intestines, which taste similar to shortbread. I have also eaten them boiled, however, most people prefer eating them raw. Intestines are a good source of fat, protein, iron, and contain some calcium and B vitamins.

The next item that Elizapea reached for was the liver. Using her ulu (semi-circular knife), my teacher cut off a bite-sized piece and ate it with relish. I followed suit and was treated to the most tender, juicy, mild-flavoured liver I have ever eaten.

A spirit of plenty is believed by some to live in the seal liver, therefore, the liver must be eaten raw in order to release the spirit back to the earth where it is passed on to the sky and eventually returns to the sea. When the spirit is kept alive and allowed to circulate throughout the land, air, and marine ecological systems, it provides a bountiful harvest to the Inuit hunters.

My gourmet guide then dismembered a limb covered with a thick layer of blubber and set it aside near the intestines. We watched as the grandfather divided the remaining carcass up among the rest of the community members. Namesakes, rather than personal preference play an important role in sharing meat. The ribs, limbs, flippers, internal organs, fat, and head parts are given to the individuals with matching namesake relationships. The eyeballs are reserved for the children.

It wasn't until I moved to Eskimo Point and happened to catch a small ringed seal in my fish net that I was able to experience eating a seal eye. Previously, I had to be satisfied with eating raw (fresh or frozen) or boiled fish eyes. Raw seal and caribou eyes are eaten by slicing the eye muscles and sucking out the internal fluid. They are also boiled along with the other head parts.

I soon learned that a well-balanced diet is maintained by eating all portions of the seal rather than limiting dietary intake to the muscle meat. Along with the intestines, the esophagus, stomach lining, stomach contents, lung, kidney, liver, heart, and head parts are delicacies that help provide vital nutrients. They are eaten raw (fresh or frozen) or boiled. One tasty combination is made by chopping together raw seal brains and blubber, creating a texture similar to whipped cream which is eaten raw.

On northern Baffin Island, summer temperatures are cool and snow can be expected at any time. The cool temperatures and few insects enable Inuit to cache meat throughout the summer. In southern arctic communities, Inuit wait until early September, after the temperature drops and the flies become dormant, before they cache their meat.

Seal fat is rendered into oil by storing it in an open glass container or a sealskin bag. I enjoyed this tangy meat dip in numerous homes and attempted to make it on my own. The results were a cloudy, foul smelling substance which I discarded under the advice of an Inuit cook. I explained what I did and everyone stated that the key to successful rendering of seal blubber was to store the fat in an open container in a shaded, cool, breezy area. Seal fat is a good source of vitamin C, A, and thiamine. Wild game is very lean, unlike domesticated meat, therefore it is necessary to include small portions of fat in one's diet.

The field season progressed and my tent became cramped with seal skins and sealskin boots in various stages of completion. My world, including my thoughts, was submerged in a seal culture.

As I walked towards the beach, looking for new seal skins, two ladies perched on the top of a five-foot-high wooden crate called out their cheery greetings. I paused for a chat and accepted their invitation to climb up and join them. I was treated to a dish akin to french fries with salt and vinegar — seal flippers soaked in blubber. The aging process breaks down the flipper's fat and gristle, transferring this gristly cut into a tender meal with a tangy, finger-licking flavour.

Caribou Inuit in the Keewatin rely on caribou rather than seal meat as their main food source. Like seal, caribou meat is eaten dried, boiled, raw, and aged.

On a spring caribou hunt I helped skin the caribou and noticed many warble fly larvae nestled just under the fascia. The hunter casually popped several into his mouth and continued skinning. I emulated his actions, realizing that these milk-coloured maggots are favourite morsels, especially among children. The mild, refreshing flavour sensation is similar to biting into a grape covered with a raspberry skin.

In the summer, most people move out to their seasonal camps. The aroma of boiling caribou meat and bones, and thoughts of warm hospitality awaiting travellers, entices visitors to trek from one camp to the next. A large cauldron of caribou bones and hooves simmering over a small fire of arctic willow and dwarf birch is a common sight at camps scattered across the tundra. The bones are cracked, hooves shelled, and the marrow, fat, and gelatin is collected, cooled, and served as a butter with bannock (biscuit-like bread) and dried meat.

As I entered Helen Paungat's tent (an Eskimo Point elder) for a visit, I noticed a caribou stomach perched neatly on a rock. Caribou stomach contents are eaten mainly by elders, young Inuit generally prefer other foods. Stomach contents are an excellent source of vitamin A and iron, and contain some vitamin B, C, calcium, and protein. This is also one of the rare sources of carbohydrates found in traditional northern diets. The mesentery fat surrounding the stomach (bridal lace) is dried and eaten as a snack with other foods.

Fresh, hard-boiled eggs, raw or boiled whale skin, boiled spring goose, dried caribou meat, dried arctic char, and tundra berries (black crowberry, alpine bear berry, bilberry, marshberry, mountain cranberry, and blueberry) are welcomed changes to the winter diet. After dinner we wiped our hands on a bird skin and a handful of grasses. Rabbit and caribou skins were also used in the past. The warm comradeship and intimate act of sharing food has continually knit together close cross-cultural relationships.

My southern eating habits are greatly influenced by my

northern teachers. Today, my favourite meals include muktuk (whale skin) and baked beans, peanut butter on dried seal meat and seal meat boiled in canned mandarins. Inuit are also combining more and more southern foods with land foods.

Today, many Inuit have jobs which take them from their home towns to large centres such as Ottawa and Montreal. Their ability to cope with a wide diversity of cultural experiences is evident as an Inuit politician climbs on the First Air connection from Igloolik to Montreal. He left Igloolik with a meal of fresh, raw, seal liver and arrived in Montreal in time to have shrimp quiche with french pastries. Inuit enthusiastically cope with the wide range of contemporary food choices; however, Inuit living in southern communities make special efforts to order fresh seal, caribou, or fish from northern land food stores in Iqaluit (Frobisher Bay) and Inuvik.

As I packed up my tent at the end of my initial arctic field trip, I realized that I would miss my diet of seal meat and assorted other tidbits. Just as Inuit occasionally ask returning travellers to bring up a fast food hamburger, I will feel the need to ask travellers returning from the arctic to bring back some land food. Subtly, Inuit women have taught me to understand that the value of food is more than cost-per-nutrient, aesthetic values, and nutrition; it is an integral part of a culture's social-psychological network.

RESPONSE

1. Why must seal liver be eaten raw?
2. Suggest reasons why the Inuit eat the entire seal.
3. What lessons has the writer learned from her Inuit teachers?

EXTENSION

4. Go to a farmers' market. Select some foods which you have never eaten. Prepare and eat the foods and report to the class on the experience.
5. Write a short story in which food in some form figures in a prominent way.

6. Browse through the cookbooks in the school resource centre. Look through them for interesting facts and recipes. Report to the class on the most interesting story and recipe.
7. Select a variety of canned, bottled, or packaged products. From the labels compile a list of unknown or unfamiliar ingredients, and find out exactly what you are ingesting.

THE HARVEST, THE KILL

JANE RULE

• What is vegetarianism?

I live among vegetarians of various persuasions and moral meat eaters; therefore when I have guests for dinner, I pay rather more attention to the nature of food than I would, left to my own imagination.

The vegetarians who don't eat meat because they believe it to be polluted with cancer-causing hormones or because they identify their sensitive digestive tracts with herbivore ancestors are just cautious folk similar to those who cross the street only at the corner with perhaps a hint of the superstition found in those who don't walk under ladders. They are simply taking special care of their lives without further moral deliberation.

Those who don't eat meat because they don't approve of killing aren't as easy for me to understand. Yesterday, as I pried live scallops from their beautiful, fragile shells and saw them still pulsing in the bowl, ready to cook for friends for whom food from the sea is acceptable, it felt to me no less absolute an act of killing than chopping off the head of a chicken. But I also know in the vegetable garden that I rip carrots untimely from their row. The fact that they don't twitch or run around without their heads doesn't make them less alive. Like me, they have grown from seed and have their own natural life span which I have interrupted. It is hard for me to be hierarchical about the aliveness of living things.

There are two vegetarian arguments that bear some guilty weight for me. The first is the number of acres it takes to feed beef cattle as compared to the number of acres it takes to feed vegetarians. If there ever were a large plan to change our basic agriculture in order to feed everyone more equably, I would support it and give up eating beef, but until then my not eating beef is of no more help than my eating my childhood dinner was to the starving Armenians. The second is mistreatment of animals raised for slaughter. To eat what has not been a free-ranging animal is to condone the abuse of animals. Again, given the opportunity to support laws for more humane treatment of the creatures we eventually eat, I would do so, but I probably wouldn't go so far as to approve of chickens so happy in life that they were tough for my table.

The moral meat eaters are those who believe that we shouldn't eat what we haven't killed ourselves, either gone to the trouble of stalking it down or raising it, so that we have proper respect for the creatures sacrificed for our benefit.

I am more at home with that view because my childhood summers were rural. By the time I was seven or eight, I had done my share of fishing and hunting, and I'd been taught also to clean my catch or kill. I never shot anything larger than a pigeon or rabbit. That I was allowed to use a gun at all was the result of a remarkably indulgent father. He never took me deer hunting, not because I was a girl but because he couldn't bear to shoot them himself. But we ate venison brought to us by other men in the family.

I don't remember much being made of the sacredness of the life we took, but there was a real emphasis on fair play, much of it codified in law, like shooting game birds only on the wing, like not hunting deer with flashlights at night, like not shooting does. But my kinfolk frowned on bait fishing as well. They were sportsmen who retained the wilderness ethic of not killing more than they could use. Strictly speaking, we did not need the food. (We could get meat in a town ten miles down the road.) But we did eat it.

Over the years, I became citified. I still could and did put live lobsters and crab in boiling water, but meat came from the meat market. Now that I live in the country again, I am much more aware of the slaughter that goes on around me, for I not only eat venison from the local hunt but have known the lamb and kid on the hoof (even in my rhododendrons, which is good for neither them nor the rhododendrons) which I eat. The killers of the animals are my moral, meat-eating neighbours. I have never killed a large animal, and I hope I never have to, though I'm not particularly tender-hearted about creatures not human. I find it hard to confront the struggle, smell, and mess of slaughter. I simply haven't the stomach for it. But, if I had to do it or go without meat, I would learn how.

It's puzzling to me that cannibalism is a fascinating abomination to vegetarian and meat eater alike, a habit claimed by only the most vicious and primitive tribes. We are scandalized by stories of the Donner Party or rumours of cannibalism at the site of a small plane crash in the wilderness, a boat lost at sea. Yet why would it be so horrifying for survivors to feed on the flesh of those who have died? Have worms and buzzards more right to the carcass?

We apparently do not think of ourselves as part of the food chain, except by cruel and exceptional accident. Our flesh, like the cow in India, is sacred and taboo, thought of as violated even when it is consigned to a mass grave. We bury it to hide a truth that still must be obvious to us, that as we eat so are we eaten. Why the lowly maggot is given the privilege (or sometimes the fish or the vulture) denied other living creatures is a complex puzzle of hygiene, myth, and morality in each culture.

Our denial that we are part of nature, our sense of superiority to it, is our basic trouble. Though we are not, as the producers of margarine would make us believe, what we eat, we are related to what we harvest and kill. If being a vegetarian or a moral meat eater is a habit to remind us of that responsibility, neither is to be disrespected. When habit becomes a taboo, it blinds us to the real meaning. We are also related to each other, but our general refusal to eat our own flesh has not stopped us from slaughtering each other in large and totally wasted numbers.

I am flesh, a flesh eater, whether the food is carrot or cow. Harvesting and killing are the same activity, the interrupting of one life cycle for the sake of another. We don't stop at eating either. We kill to keep warm. We kill for shelter.

Back there in my rural childhood, I had not only a fishing rod and rifle, I had a hatchet, too. I cleared brush, cut down small trees, chopped wood. I was present at the felling of a two-thousand-year-old redwood tree, whose impact shook the earth I stood on. It was a death more simply shocking to me than any other I've ever witnessed. The house I lived in then was made of redwood. The house I live in now is cedar.

My ashes may nourish the roots of a living tree, pitifully small compensation for the nearly immeasurable acres I have laid waste for my needs and pleasures, even for my work. For such omnivorous creatures as we are, a few frugal habits are not enough. We have to feed and midwife more than we slaughter, replant more than we harvest, if not with our hands, then with our own talents to see that it is done in our name, that we own to it.

The scallop shells will be finely cleaned by raccoons, then made by a neighbour into wind chimes, which may trouble my sleep and probably should until it is time for my own bones to sing.

RESPONSE

1. For Discussion: "Like me, they [carrots] have grown from seed and have their own natural life span which I have interrupted. It is hard for me to be hierarchical about the aliveness of living things."
2. What are the "two vegetarian arguments that bear some guilty weight" for Rule? Do you share Rule's views about these arguments? Explain.
3. What do you think the author means when she writes, "We apparently do not think of ourselves as part of the food chain, except by cruel and exceptional accident"?

EXTENSION

4. Write a letter to the editor of your local newspaper taking as your theme Rule's assertion that "Our denial that we are part of nature, our sense of superiority to it, is our basic trouble."
5. Write a short poem or prose piece entitled "Reverence."

HOW TO COOK A CARP

EUELL GIBBONS

• What are the pros and cons of sport fishing?

---

hen I was a lad of about eighteen, my brother and I were working on a cattle ranch in New Mexico that bordered on the Rio Grande. Most Americans think of the Rio Grande as a warm southern stream, but it rises among the high mountains of Colorado, and in the spring it is fed by melting snows. At this time of the year, the water that rushed by the ranch was turbulent, icy-cold and so silt-laden as to be semisolid. "A little too thick to drink, and a little too thin to plow" was a common description of the waters of the Rio Grande.

A few species of fish inhabited this muddy water. Unfortunately, the most common was great eight- to ten-pound carp, a fish that is considered very poor eating in this country, although the Germans and Asiatics have domesticated this fish, and have developed some varieties that are highly esteemed for the table.

On the ranch where we worked, there was a drainage ditch that ran through the lower pasture and emptied its clear waters into the muddy Rio Grande. The carp swimming up the river would strike this clear warmer water and decide they preferred it to the cold mud they had been inhabiting. One spring day, a cowhand who had been riding that way reported that Clear Ditch was becoming crowded with huge carp.

On Sunday we decided to go fishing. Four of us armed ourselves with pitchforks, saddled our horses and set out. Near the mouth of

the ditch, the water was running about two feet deep and twelve
to sixteen feet wide. There is a saying in that part of the country
that you can't get a cowboy to do anything unless it can be done
from the back of a horse, so we forced our mounts into the ditch
and started wading them upstream, four abreast, herding the carp
before us.

By the time we had ridden a mile upstream, the water was less
than a foot deep and so crystal clear that we could see our herd of
several hundred carp still fleeing from the splashing, wading
horses. As the water continued to shallow, our fish began to get
panicky. A few of the boldest ones attempted to dart back past us
and were impaled on pitchforks. We could see that the whole herd
was getting restless and was about to stampede back downstream,
so we piled off our horses into the shallow water to meet the
charge. The water boiled about us as the huge fish swirled past us
and we speared madly in every direction with our pitchforks,
throwing each fish we managed to hit over the ditch bank. This
was real fishing — cowhand style. The last of the fish herd was by
us in a few minutes and it was all over, but we had caught a
tremendous quantity of fish.

Back at the ranch house, after we had displayed our trophies,
we began wondering what we were going to do with so many fish.
This started a series of typical cowboy tall tales on "how to cook
a carp." The best of these yarns was told by a grizzled old
vaquero, who claimed he had made his great discovery when he
ran out of food while camping on a tributary of the Rio Grande.
He said that he had found the finest way to cook a carp was to
plaster the whole fish with a thick coating of fresh cow manure
and bury it in the hot ashes of a campfire. In an hour or two, he
said, the casing of cow manure had become black and very hard.
He then related how he had removed the fish from the fire, broken
the hard shell with the butt of his Winchester and peeled it off. He
said that as the manure came off the scales and skin adhered to it,
leaving the baked fish, white and clean. He then ended by saying,
"Of course, the carp still wasn't fit to eat, but the manure in which
it was cooked tasted pretty good."

There were also some serious suggestions and experiments. The
chief objection to the carp is that its flesh is full of many forked
bones. One man said that he had enjoyed carp sliced very thin
and fried so crisp that one could eat it, bones and all. He

demonstrated, and you really could eat it without the bones bothering you, but it was still far from being an epicurean dish. One cowboy described the flavor as "a perfect blend of Rio Grande mud and rancid hog lard."

Another man said that he had eaten carp that had been cooked in a pressure cooker until the bones softened and became indistinguishable from the flesh. A pressure cooker is almost a necessity at that altitude, so we had one at the ranch house. We tried this method and the result was barely edible. It tasted like the poorest possible grade of canned salmon flavored with a bit of mud. It was, however, highly appreciated by the dogs and cats on the ranch, and solved the problem of what to do with the bulk of the fish we had caught.

It was my brother who finally devised a method of cooking carp that not only made it fit for human consumption, but actually delicious. First, instead of merely scaling the fish, he skinned them. Then, taking a large pinch where the meat was thickest, he worked his fingers and thumb into the flesh until he struck the median bones, then he worked his thumb and fingers together and tore off a handful of meat. Using this tearing method, he could get two or three good-sized chunks of flesh from each side of the fish. He then heated a pot of bland vegetable shortening, rubbed the pieces of fish with salt and dropped them into the hot fat. He used no flour, meal, crumbs or seasoning other than salt. They cooked to a golden brown in a few minutes, and everyone pronounced them "mighty fine eating." The muddy flavor seemed to have been eliminated by removing the skin and the large bones. The forked bones were still there, but they had not been multiplied by cutting across them, and one only had to remove several bones still intact with the fork from each piece of fish.

For the remainder of that spring, every few days one or another of the cowboys would take a pitchfork and ride over to Clear Ditch and spear a mess of carp. On these evenings, my brother replaced the regular *cocinero* and we enjoyed some delicious fried carp.

The flavor of carp varies with the water from which it is caught. Many years after the above incidents I attended a fish fry at my brother's house. The main course was all of his own catching, and consisted of bass, catfish, and carp, all from Elephant Butte Lake farther down the Rio Grande. All the fish were prepared exactly alike, except that the carp was pulled apart as described above, while the bass and catfish, being all twelve inches or less in length, were merely cleaned and fried whole. None of his guests knew one fish from another, yet all of them preferred the carp to the other kinds. These experiences have convinced me that the carp is really a fine food fish when properly prepared.

Carp can, of course, be caught in many ways besides spearing them with pitchforks from the back of a horse. In my adopted home state, Pennsylvania, they are classed as "trash fish" and one is allowed to take them almost any way. They will sometimes bite on worms, but they are vegetarians by preference and are more easily taken on dough balls. Some states allow the use of gill nets, and other states, because they would like to reduce the population of this unpopular fish, will issue special permits for the use of nets to catch carp.

A good forager will take advantage of the lax regulations on carp fishing while they last. When all fisherman realize that the carp is really a good food fish when prepared in the right way, maybe this outsized denizen of our rivers and lakes will no longer be considered a pest and will take his rightful place among our valued food and game fishes.

RESPONSE

1. Why do you think the cowboys went after the carp in the first place when they had no intention of eating them?
2. How do you think Wendell Berry ("Know That What You Eat You Are") would respond to the cowboys' behaviour?

EXTENSION

3. Talk to some local sport fishing enthusiasts. Ask them about their attitude to the sport and to the fish.
4. For Discussion: What is the value of sport fishing? You might wish to consider some of the following questions:
   a) Does sport fishing contribute to conservation?
   b) Is the use of fish justified for entertainment?

GRIFFIN

THE WAYS OF WATER

THE DAY NIAGARA FALLS RAN DRY

DAVID PHILLIPS

- Why is Niagara Falls considered to be one of the wonders of the natural world?

O n the night of March 29, 1848, the unthinkable happened. The mighty Niagara Falls eased to a trickle and then fell silent for 30 puzzling hours. It was the only known time this wonder of the world has ever been stilled. So incredible was the event that 30 years later eyewitnesses were asked to swear signed declarations that they were there when "the Falls of Niagara ran dry."

Residents first realized something was wrong when they were awakened by an overpowering silence. Inspection of the river by torches revealed only a few puddles of water in the riverbed. The next morning some 5,000 sightseers converged on the riverbank to see the phenomenon. The American Falls had slowed to a trickle, the British Channel was drying fast, and the thundering

Canadian Horseshoe Falls were stilled. Upriver at Chippewa, the Welland River was reduced to a tiny stream. Above the falls water wheels at flour mills and factories stopped turning as the river level dropped.

For some the event was an interesting curiosity. Inspection of the river revealed long stretches of drying mud, boulders and chains of blackened puddles. Fish and turtles lay floundering in crevices. While thousands stood in disbelief, a few daredevils explored recesses and cavities never before exposed at the bottom of the dry river gorge. They picked up bayonets, muskets, swords, gun barrels, tomahawks and other relics of the War of 1812. Some young entrepreneurs drove a cart onto the exposed riverbed just above the Canadian falls to retrieve huge pine timbers. Years later, owners of furniture made from those once-submerged timbers delighted in recalling how the wood was obtained.

Below the falls, the dry river course provided an opportunity to blast out the rocks that had always scraped the keel of the *Maid of the Mist.* As one account stated, "The canyon of the river reverberated to constant blasting as the rocks were blown to pieces and removed with the same ease as if they had been on dry land."

For others, though, the unusual silence and unexplained phenomenon was a portent of divine wrath or impending doom. As the day wore on, fear and anxiety spread. Thousands attended special church services on both sides of the border. Indians shared in the superstition that some disaster was about to happen.

Tension grew until the night of March 31, when a low growl from upstream announced the return of the waters. Suddenly, a "wall" of water surged down the riverbed and over the falls. The deluge quickly restored the ever-present Niagara mist. Relieved residents relaxed and returned home to sleep once again to the rumble and boom of the falls.

The cause of the stoppage, it was discovered later, was an ice jam on Lake Erie near Buffalo. In an average winter, Lake Erie is almost completely ice-covered. Normally, by the end of March the lake is clear except in the eastern basin near Buffalo where prevailing winds and water currents concentrate drifting ice. Westerly winds blowing down nearly 400 kilometres of open water break the ice into mammoth chunks and remould it into ridges and rafted ice.

Contrary to published reports, the winter of 1847-48 had not been intensely cold and Lake Erie's ice cover was not thicker than the usual 10 to 60 centimetres. In fact, the winter was about two degrees milder than usual, although the first half of March was unseasonably cold. In late March 1848, several days of stiff easterly winds drove Erie's pack ice up the lake. But on March 29, the winds suddenly reversed direction, coming out of the southwest and west and propelling the vast ice field back down the lake. The ice was melting rapidly as afternoon temperatures went to 7°C under clear skies. The combined force of wind, waves and lake currents jammed hundreds of thousands of tonnes of ice into a solid dam at the neck of the lake and the river entrance between Fort Erie and Buffalo.

The weather continued balmy, however, and nighttime temperatures stayed above freezing. On March 31 the temperature rose to 16°C, the winds continued to shift and strengthen, and that night the Niagara ice wedge dislodged, restoring the river flow.

Will Niagara Falls ever run dry again? Probably not, at least not on its own accord. Since 1964, an ice boom has been positioned at the head of the Niagara River every winter to prevent the formation of ice blockages and safeguard hydroelectric installations.

For seven months in 1969, the U.S. Army Corps of Engineers turned off the American Falls by diverting the river to permit repairs to the eroding face of the falls. On at least five other occasions the American Falls have frozen over completely, but not the Canadian Horseshoe Falls. With 10 times the volume of the American Falls, only once has its mighty roar been stilled — 141 years ago on that memorable March night.

RESPONSE

1. Apart from the actual stopping of the flow of the river, what were some of the surprises that occurred when the falls ran dry?
2. Why was it possible for Niagara Falls to run dry in 1848, but unlikely that it will ever run dry again?

3. Imagine you were a resident around Niagara Falls at the end of March, 1848. Write a journal account of your activities and how they were affected by the "drying up" of the falls.
4. Write a short piece about an unusual natural event in your own area.

THE POWER OF A RAINDROP

GARRY LAWRENCE FAIRBAIRN

- In your group, recount an experience with rain that was particularly impressive in some way.
- What do you know about the rain patterns in your area?

Raindrops that seem to be flowing normally on loose cultivated soil often have bursts of speed over distances of several millimeters, sucking minute soil particles into their wake. First to go are the lightest particles, which are generally particles of organic matter that both nourish plants and help bind the soil together. Individual falling raindrops also have substantial impact, sometimes splashing soil particles one meter vertically and two meters horizontally on unsheltered soil surfaces. The potential effects of rain do not end there. In addition to drawing soil away over the surface, rain can seal and compact the soil, starting a vicious circle of ever-worsening erosion. The compacted soil is less able to absorb water, thus increasing water flow and the rate at which surface matter is carried away. The soil also becomes more vulnerable to compaction by heavy machinery.

The worst impact of erosion currently is in the Maritime Provinces, where some potato farmers are struggling to squeeze production out of pathetically small remnants of topsoil. New Brunswick farmers have been hardest hit, since their soils were comparatively shallow from the beginning. The deeper topsoils of Prince Edward Island have sheltered potato farmers there, but similar problems could confront the island in a decade or two.

Ironically, the same potato crop that has been an economic blessing to the low-income Maritime Provinces has been the soil's worst enemy. And the modern agricultural technology that gave a boost to many farmers now threatens their land, under present use of that technology. In the upper St. John River valley, where potato acreage and specialization in potatoes has increased markedly since 1945, soil erosion rates in studied areas have increased by more than five times. In pre-specialization days, more grasses and legume plants were grown, providing almost continuous vegetative cover to the soil. The roots and other residues of grasses and legumes returned much organic matter to the soil, helping bind soil particles together in a stronger soil structure. But, with concentration on wide-row crops like potatoes and corn, stresses increased. Because such crops must be resown annually, the land stands bare and exposed for longer periods of the year. And, in the gaps between rows of plants, water can flow unobstructed, carrying with it the soil. For one veteran New Brunswick soil scientist, Kenneth Langmaid, all the examples of destroyed fields and shattered hopes were symbolized in an abandoned plow he noticed one day. Some years previously, a farmer had obviously hitched up his horses to the hand-guided plow and had done just a few furrows before giving up forever in despair. Behind the derelict plow, Langmaid could still see the soft rotten shale-bed rock that it had turned up. The area had been settled for a century, but intensively cultivated in potatoes for only fifteen years.

Despite the stresses placed on the soil by potato production, some Maritimes farms have had no proper crop rotation, manure application, or other conservation practices in thirty years. Some farmers, in fact, have squeezed potatoes out of the same field continuously for more than a quarter century. Rows of plants can be seen running straight down slopes of twelve degrees or more, presenting not even a wisp of a barrier to water runoff. On the sandy loam and loam soils of Prince Edward Island, where continuous potato and corn production has created severe compaction, scientists have found serious erosion even on gentle three-degree slopes. Altogether, water erosion is considered a serious potential problem on 75 percent of the Maritime region's agricultural lands. Annual losses of twenty tonnes of soil per hectare are common in the potato-producing lands of New Brunswick and Prince Edward Island. Some estimates put the New Brunswick loss at an appalling forty-two tonnes per hectare. Here and there, visual signs of the loss can be found — for example, where hedgerows have protected the soil underneath, the ground can be two-thirds of a meter higher than in adjacent eroded fields.

In Ontario and Quebec, continuous cropping of corn and soybeans has also brought severe erosion problems in recent years. Water erosion alone takes the equivalent of 6,000 hectares, to a depth of fifteen centimeters, from Ontario farmlands each year. The average soil loss through erosion in southern Ontario is just under 5.4 tonnes per hectare each year. Where corn is grown continuously on sloping land, however, the loss is far worse than that average. Cases have been documented in southern Ontario and in Quebec's eastern townships where erosion losses surpassed 50 tonnes a hectare — a loss of more topsoil in a single year than even the fastest natural processes can create in four years. Ontario scientists consider annual erosion losses of 7 tonnes per hectare as the maximum amount that can be tolerated without reducing crop yields.

RESPONSE

1. In what ways have some farming methods contributed to soil erosion?
2. Why do you think some farmers do not adopt comprehensive practices to inhibit erosion?

EXTENSION

3. For Discussion: What do you think will be some of the consequences of the erosion process if it is allowed to continue at the present rate?
4. Research and write a short paper on rainfall in your area.

WHY AND WHEN WE SEE RAINBOWS

DAVID PHILLIPS

- In your group, list all of the associations you know concerning rainbows. Why do you think there are so many?

Many people consider the rainbow to be the most magnificent of all sky phenomena. Its appearance has inspired artists, poets and composers throughout the ages. In many cultures, notably the Irish, the rainbow was believed to be magic and a token of good fortune. Although the ancients attributed the rainbow to gods and witches and the Greeks saw it as a sign of war and death, several cultures revered it as a symbol of renewed hope. In the Bible, the rainbow is a reminder that God will never again flood the whole earth. Indeed, a rainbow often is a sign that the rain has ended.

A rainbow is merely sunlight. There is nothing material or physical about it, only an optical illusion like a mirage or a halo. How do rainbows form? Why is it they only occur sometimes when the sun shines during a rainstorm? Can they happen at night, or be used to forecast the weather?

To see a rainbow, the proper angle must be set up between the sun, a curtain of rain and you, the observer. In other words, you must face the rain with the sun at your back; a rainbow cannot be formed if the sky is completely obscured by cloud. If a rainbow appears, it will be at a 42° angle up from your shadow.

This positioning — back to the sun while facing a shower — is the basis for the old adage that says a morning rainbow is a warning of foul weather, while an afternoon or evening rainbow promises clear skies. This bit of weather lore relies on the usual west-to-east movement of weather systems in the mid-latitudes. Thus, if a rainbow is seen in the morning when the sun is to the east of where you stand, the shower responsible for the rainbow must be to the west, and is likely moving towards you. On the other hand, if a rainbow is in the east in the afternoon or evening, then rain has passed by and will continue to recede eastward, giving way to clearing skies from the west.

Raindrops act like miniature prisms and mirrors splitting light into a spectrum of colours from violet to red, and then reflecting those colours. Whether you see bright bands of colour depends on the angle at which the white sunlight strikes the surface of a raindrop. Part of the light is reflected and part of it enters the drop, where it is twice refracted, or bent, and once reflected.

The first refraction takes place when the light enters the drop and disperses into colours. On entry, the speed of the ray of light is slowed; in fact, each colour of light is slowed at a different rate and thus bent at a slightly different angle. Violet light travels the slowest and is curved the most. Red travels the fastest and is bent the least. When it reaches the opposite side of the drop, the light is partially reflected off the inside back, and then is refracted again on leaving from the same side it entered. The angle between the entering sunlight and the exiting rainbow rays varies from 42° for red light to about 40° for violet light.

The geometry involved in the formation of rainbows means that those viewed from the ground, when the sun is just above the horizon, will appear as semicircles. The higher the sun is in the sky, the smaller the rainbow, disappearing altogether for someone on the ground when the sun is at an altitude of 42° above the horizon. A full-circle rainbow is rarely seen, and at that is usually only visible from an airplane when the sun is high in the sky and reflecting off a curtain of rain. Well-defined, bright rainbows are usually associated with large raindrops.

Each raindrop disperses the full spectrum of colours, but you will see only a single colour from each raindrop, depending on the angle of the sunlight and your position. It takes millions of falling drops — each refracting and reflecting light back to your eyes at slightly different angles — to produce the continuous coloured bands of the rainbow. While each drop falls, another takes its place in your line of vision, until the number of raindrops begins to diminish and the rainbow fades. The foot of the rainbow is its brightest spot, where the seven colours — violet, indigo, blue, green, yellow, orange and red — blend into a yellowish "pot of gold."

Each person sees his or her own personal rainbow. While two people may admire the beauty of a rainbow together, what they see is not exactly the same since each person views sunlight dispersed from a different set of raindrops.

Sometimes, when a bright rainbow is visible, a second, larger rainbow can be seen parallel to the first. The secondary bow happens when sunlight enters the raindrops at a specific angle that allows light to make two reflections inside the raindrop instead of one. Thus the secondary bow is larger and is positioned above the primary one.

Light emerging from the secondary bow is always fainter because each reflection weakens the intensity. Colours in the outer rainbow are in the reverse order to those in the primary rainbow with red on the inside and violet on the outside. As many as three or more rainbows can form, but they are usually too faint to be seen. With each additional reflection, there is a reversal of the previous order of colours.

Honolulu, Hawaii is famous for its brilliant rainbows, but at Niagara Falls, visitors are almost always treated to coloured arcs in the mist, as long as the sun is shining. But one does not have to travel far to view a rainbow. Miniature coloured arches can be seen in the mist of water sprinklers, fountains and waterfalls, in the splash of a boat's bow wave, or in spray thrown up on a wet road.

In southern Canada, the most spectacular rainbows are seen most frequently in summer since there are more showers and thunderstorms then, usually in the early morning or late afternoon. Do not look for a rainbow at noon, though. At midday, when the sun is more than 42° above the horizon, the bow is cut off from sight because the reflected light from the raindrops passes above your head.

Similarly, chasing rainbows does not bring you any closer to them. A rainbow is as near or as far as the raindrops reflecting the sunlight. If you walk towards a rainbow, you will not be able to look up and see it over your head; it may or may not still be seen in the distance.

Rainbows can occasionally occur on clear moonlit nights in the same way as the more common daytime rainbows. However, since the light from the moon is dimmer than the sun's, lunar rainbows, or moonbows, are noticeably fainter and more difficult to see.

RESPONSE

1. How can rainbows be used to predict the weather?
2. Why is it impossible to walk under a rainbow?
3. Why are rainbows in the form of an arch?

EXTENSION

4. Write a myth about the origin of rainbows. Dramatize your myth.
5. Investigate the phenomenon of "sun dogs" and "moon dogs."

WATERWORKS

EMILY CARR

- To your group, recount an experience which you may have had at an "unplumbed" cottage or at home when the plumbing failed.
- Where does your community's fresh water come from?

Those Victorians [people of Victoria] who did not have a well on their own place bought water by the bucket from the great barrel water-cart which peddled it.

Water brought in wooden pipes from Spring Ridge on the northern outskirts of the town was our next modernness. Three wonderful springs watered Victoria, one on Spring Ridge, one in Fairfield and one at Beacon Hill. People carried this sparkling deliciousness in pails from whichever spring was nearest their home.

My father was so afraid of fire that he dug many wells on his land and had also two great cisterns for soft water. Everyone had a rain barrel or two at the corners of his house. The well under our kitchen was deep and had a spring at the bottom. Two pumps stood side by side in our kitchen. One was for well water and one was a cistern pump — water from the former was hard and clear, from the cistern it was brownish and soft.

When Beaver Lake water was piped into Victoria, everyone had taps put in their kitchen and it was a great event. House walls burst into lean-to additions with vent pipes piercing their roofs. These were new bathrooms. With the coming of the water system came sewerage. The wretched little "privies" in every backyard folded their evil wings and flapped away — Victoria had at last outgrown them and was going stylish and modern.

Father built a beautiful bathroom. Two sides of it were of glass. It was built over the verandah and he trained his grape-vine round the windows. The perfume of the vine in spring poured through the open windows deliciously. Father had tried to build several bathrooms before Beaver Lake came to town, but none of them had been any good. First he used a small north room and had a cistern put up in the attic to fill the bathtub. But hot water had to be lugged upstairs in a bucket and anyway the cistern froze every winter; so that bathroom was a failure. He had made us an enormous, movable wooden tub like a baby's bath big enough for a grown-up to lie in flat. It was very heavy and lived on the back verandah. Bong brought it into the kitchen on Saturday nights before he left for town. It had to be filled and emptied over and over by the ladies of the household with a long-handled dipper until all the family had had their baths. Besides this Saturday night monster there were wooden wash tubs painted white which lived under our beds. We pulled these out at night and filled them with cold water. Into this we were supposed to plunge every morning. This was believed to harden us; if your nose were not blue enough at the breakfast table to guarantee that you had plunged, there was trouble.

Father later tried a bathroom off the wash-house across the yard. A long tin pipe hung under the chin of the wash-house pump and carried cold water, but hot water had to be dipped out of the wash boiler on the stove. This hot bath arrangement was bad; we got cold crossing the yard afterwards. So the wooden tub was invited into the kitchen again each Saturday night until we became "plumbed."

It was glorious having Beaver Lake pour out of taps in your kitchen and we gloated at being plumbed. Mothers were relieved to see wells filled in, to be rid of the constant anxiety of their children falling in and being well-drowned. Everyone was proud and happy about this plumbing until the first hard frost.

Victoria used to have very cold winters. There was always some skating and some sleighing and spells of three or four days at a time when the wind from the north would pierce everything. Mother's milk pans in the dairy froze solid. We chopped ice-cream off the top to eat with our morning porridge. Meat froze, bread froze, everything in the house froze although the big hall stove was red hot and there were three or four roaring grate fires as well. Windows were frosted in beautiful patterns all day and our breath smoked.

It was then discovered that plumbers, over-driven by the rush of modern arrangements, had neglected to protect the pipes from frost. Most of the bathrooms were built on the north side of the houses and everything froze except our deep kitchen well. Neighbours rushed to the Carr pump, spilling new snow over Mother's kitchen floor till our house was one great puddle and the kitchen was filled with the icy north wind. Everyone suddenly grumbled at modern plumbing. When the thaw came and all the pipes burst everyone wished Beaver Lake could be piped right back to where it came from.

RESPONSE

1. What were the different kinds of water available to Emily Carr? What use do you think would be made of these different kinds of water?
2. What changes in lifestyle did Beaver Lake water bring about?

EXTENSION

3. Do you think people are still "over-driven by the rush of modern arrangements"? Explain.
4. Investigate the source, the treatment, and the levels of consumption of your community's water. Report your findings to the class.

AH, SWEET SEWAGE LAGOON!

Y. ROBERT TYMSTRA

- How is waste water treated in your community?
- Are there any environmental hazards associated with this treatment?

A migrating flock of sandpipers wings over the patchwork scenery of southwestern Ontario. Farmlands and woodlots pass below, broken occasionally by urban sprawl. Suddenly, a glint of open water appears and the weary birds descend. They circle once and land on the shore of a shallow pond dotted with clumps of cattails. Farther along the bank other shorebirds are feeding and a great blue heron stalks quietly for unwary prey. A muskrat makes repairs to its lodge as ducks paddle nearby. Turtles and frogs bask on floating debris and the air is alive with the sound of gurgling marsh wrens, screaming blackbirds and cackling coots. The sandpipers have stopped to rest — at a sewage lagoon!

Images of smelly cesspools devoid of life may leap to mind, but many of these ponds are actually attractive wetland communities in which a myriad of wild creatures thrive, from tiny bacteria to white-tailed deer. Moreover, sewage lagoons normally smell surprisingly good.

More properly called biological oxidation ponds or waste stabilization ponds, sewage lagoons are the simplest and most natural way of treating domestic wastes. Through the action of bacteria, air and sunlight, organic material in the sewage is digested, leaving water that is 99.5 percent pollution free and clean enough to be drained into nearby rivers and lakes.

Sewage lagoons serve more than a thousand communities across Canada. They range in size from tiny single ponds, such as the one in Manyberries, Alta. (population 62), to the huge multi-lagoon complex in Kamloops, B.C. (population 64,000). Even as far north as Tuktoyaktuk, N.W.T., these ponds are a mainstay of sewage treatment.

A typical medium-sized lagoon system is that of Brights Grove, Ont., a village northeast of Sarnia near the southern end of Lake Huron. Each day the community of 2500 persons pumps roughly 1,000 cubic metres of sewage into one of its three six-hectare ponds a kilometre away. Earthen dikes contain the sewage within the artificial excavations. Remnants of silver maple swamp and hawthorn scrub surround the lagoons and keep them well hidden. Local nature enthusiasts know about them, however, and often can be seen observing some of the dozens of species of lagoon inhabitants.

The creation of this wildlife oasis begins in the toilets, kitchens and laundry rooms of Brights Grove. Wastes are flushed and drained away — out of sight and mind — into the village's sewers, whence they are collected at a pump station and sent as a milky-grey fluid to the ponds.

Here nature takes over and the purification process begins. In a few months the liquid can be discharged directly into Lake Huron.

In the Brights Grove lagoons both aerobic (requiring oxygen) and anaerobic (oxygen absent) processes are present; some community ponds have only one component. Aerobic activity takes place in the upper layer of the pond. The decomposition begins with bacteria found naturally in the sewage and soil. Wind and wave action oxygenate the water, enabling these bacteria to begin feeding on organic matter in the sewage and break it down into simpler compounds of nitrogen, phosphorus, potassium and carbon dioxide. All of these are of high nutrient value for the growth of algae. In the presence of sunlight, algae begin photosynthesizing and produce oxygen which stimulates further bacterial activity. More bacteria produce more carbon dioxide which, in turn, sustains the algae's life cycle, and so on. This mutually beneficial relationship between bacteria and algae enables a rapid and complete breakdown of sewage.

Undigested organic material and dead bacteria and algae settle to the bottom where little or no oxygen exists. Here anaerobic bacteria slowly break down the accumulated substances, producing acids, methane and carbon dioxide. In winter, ice at the surface prevents sufficient sunlight and oxygen from entering the water and the whole lagoon becomes anaerobic. When the ice melts in the spring, some typical sewage odours may be produced by anaerobic compounds but soon disappear as the pond "goes aerobic" once again.

In southern Ontario, clear, fresh water usually results in one to three months, by which time most of the bio-chemical oxygen demand (BOD) and 99 percent of disease-causing agents have been removed. (BOD is a measure of the oxygen used by decomposing organic solids that, if discharged directly to a body of water, cause pollution by stimulating algal growth.)

Bacteria and algae are the base of the pyramid of life in the lagoon. Preying on these life forms is an incredible array of tiny organisms, from microscopic single-celled protozoans to small crustaceans such as the abundant daphnia (a water flea). In the bottom sludge, nematodes (roundworms) and other small invertebrates digest solid organic matter not readily broken down by other organisms. These creatures become food for insects such as water beetles and midge larvae, which are in turn eaten by frogs, turtles and ducks. Herons and raccoons are among the top predators of this complex food chain fuelled by sewage.

Sewage lagoons are relatively cheap and easy to build and, consequently, have become popular all over the world. Once they are in operation, they practically run themselves. The main disadvantages to their use are the time it takes for the purification process and the large amounts of land required. Where time and space are available, however, lagoons are a viable alternative to more sophisticated sewage treatment facilities. In addition to being almost odourless if managed properly, they do not add to noise pollution and they run on solar energy. The biological processes even contribute some oxygen to the atmosphere.

Furthermore, any accumulated sludge that may need to be dredged can be used as an agricultural soil conditioner. Nothing goes to waste.

While toxins and industrial spills can quickly destroy the treatment capabilities of a modern sewage plant, sewage lagoons, with their larger volumes, provide operators with more time to react and correct problems before all the bacteria are destroyed. Cattails (often referred to as nature's kidneys) and other aquatic plants filter out many toxic substances before the water is released.

Lagoons can be relocated more easily than conventional plants if land costs become a factor. As well, expansion of treatment capacity is possible by simply building more ponds or adding mechanical aerators to speed up the bacterial process. They can even be used by large metropolitan areas given sufficient land.

Chris Brook manages the Brights Grove lagoons, which are under the jurisdiction of the Ontario Ministry of the Environment. Among his tasks are monitoring water quality and keeping the bacteria healthy. These lagoons have needed little maintenance since their construction in 1976 and no chemical treatments (to cure such ailments as algal blooms or high levels of particulate matter or excessive phosphates) have ever been necessary. As long as the lagoons are fed the domestic wastes they are designed for, they will operate smoothly. They are not meant to take hazardous industrial effluents.

On occasion, however, more than sewage enters the system. Bar screens at the main pumps stop larger objects, such as bicycle frames, pieces of lumber and tires, but smaller items and substances slip through and end up in the lagoons. While these usually are no more than a visual annoyance, large amounts of crankcase oil, for instance, can hamper the biological processes; small amounts of toxic chemicals do not.

A full pond is retained for a minimum of three months at Brights Grove. Water samples are regularly analyzed for levels of suspended solids, phosphates and heavy metals. When a full pond passes the test, it is gravity fed into a nearby creek that drains into Lake Huron. The "dump" takes three days and is monitored throughout the period. Because the discharge may discolour the lake and contain some coliform bacteria, this phase is done in the early spring or late fall when recreational use of the lake is low.

Controlling water levels can be a challenge. When the system was first built, Brook says, it took from five to six months to fill a pond to its maximum 1.5-metre depth. Brights Grove has been rapidly expanding, however, and filling now takes just under three months, the minimum recommended time for retention. So far, the lagoons have been working well under the increased load, but a fourth pond may soon be necessary.

Brook juggles the water levels in each of the ponds so that one may be filling, another draining and yet another in retention. For wildlife, this is generally a blessing. Varied water levels create different habitats, each attracting a particular set of inhabitants. Among birds, for instance, migrating sea ducks and loons prefer the deep open reservoirs; a shallow (less than one metre deep) lagoon overgrown with cattails may host blackbirds, rails and coots; while recently drained ones with exposed mudflats and pools are rife with a variety of shorebirds.

No two ponds are alike and even the same lagoon may vary from month to month. Water levels rise and fall like long-period tides and habitats can change dramatically. Sometimes, this means floating nests are grounded, leaving eggs or young birds exposed to predators. It's a risk the waterfowl take. Sudden changes, however, are reserved for the spring and fall, before and after the nesting season.

Risk does not seem to be a factor in the health of wildlife inhabiting the sewage ponds. John Archer, municipal pollution officer for the provincial ministry, says he has not seen any effects on wild creatures from contaminants in the lagoons. In fact, he says ducks love the lagoons and face more danger from hunters in the fall than from contamination in the water. He adds that while undoubtedly there will be trace amounts of heavy metals and other pollutants in the lagoons, he has not seen any ill effects from these sources either. Indeed, he recounts incidents of regional inspectors having fallen into the ponds while checking intake pipes, and no one became sick. If the lagoons are run properly, he says, the contaminant level is low.

The passing seasons exert their influence on the sewage lagoons too. Some wild creatures live their entire lives here; others come only to visit. The atmosphere is one of constant change.

Dawn in late spring is perhaps the most beautiful time at the Brights Grove lagoons — and the noisiest. Red-winged blackbirds and killdeers scream at intruders near their nests. Toads trill; leopard frogs give their "snoring" call and green frogs their banjo strum. In the shallower ponds, duckweed covers much of the surface in a luxuriant green mat, and islands of cattails and bulrushes harbour nests. Newly hatched ducks and coots, escorted by parents, fill every corner. A white-tailed deer treads nimbly in the shallows, nibbling tender shoots. A kingbird snaps up a damselfly. Half a dozen painted turtles, the scavengers of these waters, bask on floating debris, ready to slide into the safety of the lagoon at the first sign of danger. Pairs of iridescent-winged dragonflies dart about in tandem as they mate. Water striders and whirligig beetles skate on the quiet surface waters. Diving beetles, dragonfly nymphs, water fleas and snails are just a small part of an equally diverse underwater world.

This sheer exuberance of life quiets down somewhat in summer. Now young birds are dispersing and migrants beginning to arrive. The first groups of southbound shorebirds stop to rest and feed. Twittering swallows course over the ponds, catching insects on the wing. Swallowtail and sulphur butterflies flutter along the banks overgrown with alfalfa and mustards, while in the vegetation below, praying mantises and wolf spiders hunt.

As autumn arrives, more shorebirds stop in from the north. The yellowlegs — large sandpipers that act as sentinels — occasionally pipe out shrill alarms and the nervous shorebirds fly off, circling the lagoons in tight formations. More often than not, there seems to be no apparent reason for their flight, but sometimes a peregrine falcon or merlin sails over, justifying the panic. Soon they settle again and continue probing the rich sludge for invertebrates as they build up fat reserves for the long migration south. As the first frost sets in, northern ducks, including buffleheads, scaups and scoters, join the large flocks of adult and juvenile coots. Many will stay until the ponds begin to freeze.

The lagoons are silent in winter. The bare trees do little to shelter the ponds from the cold north winds blowing off Lake Huron. Beneath the ice, bacteria are still processing, though more slowly now. Dead cattails and reeds poke through the snow drifts. Raccoon and fox tracks criss-cross the virgin snow. A muskrat has kept a hole open in the ice and feeds on some dredged-up cattail roots. Overhead, a red-tailed hawk soars on a chilly thermal, scanning the landscape for mice and rabbits.

About the middle of March, male red-winged blackbirds arrive at the still-frozen ponds to begin proclaiming their territories from the tops of cattail flags. With the first thaw, drakes of a dozen species of waterfowl are vying for the attention of females with courtship dances and calls. Sandpipers restlessly feed before the last leg of their journey to their arctic and subarctic breeding grounds. From the adjacent woodlands, orioles and thrushes whistle their melodious songs. Life has come full circle.

The value of sewage lagoons to wild things is inestimable. Natural wetlands across the country have been drained and reclaimed for developing farmlands and cities, and as a result many forms of life are now threatened. In southwestern Ontario, 90 percent of the original wetlands have already been destroyed. In areas where sewage lagoons are the only wet areas to be found (especially in times of drought), they have become important refuges for many water-loving creatures. Indeed, some uncommon birds — Wilson's phalarope, pintail and ruddy duck — may actually be expanding their breeding range due to the presence of lagoons.

Our society produces a steadily increasing volume of domestic sewage, industrial effluents and agricultural wastes. The sewage lagoon is a simple, natural method of absorbing some of these wastes without endangering the health and well-being of man or nature. And, unwittingly, the same wastes have contributed to an all-too-rare success story for wetland wildlife.

RESPONSE

1. What advantages do sewage lagoons have over conventional treatment plants?
2. What are the disadvantages of sewage lagoons?
3. Why do you think there are not more sewage lagoons in this country?

EXTENSION

4. a) Arrange a field trip to the water treatment facility in your community.

b) Write a report outlining the procedures the facility follows.

c) In your report be sure to make some recommendations about the ways in which the process could be improved.

d) Send a copy of your report to the local water authority.

5. Invite a member of your local water authority to your class to talk about whether a sewage lagoon would work in your community.

LETTERS FROM HEAVEN

JAY INGRAM

• How would you describe snow to someone who has never seen it?

In February 1635, the philosopher and scientist René Descartes was in Amsterdam for a couple of snowy days, and his descriptions of the snowflakes he saw have never been bettered:

". . . what astonished me most was that among the grains which fell last I noticed some which had around them six little teeth, like clockmaker's wheels . . .

. . . on the morning of the following day, [there were] little plates of ice, very flat, very polished, very transparent, but so perfectly formed in hexagons that it is impossible for men to make anything so exact . . ,

. . . There followed after this little crystal columns, decorated at each end with a six-petalled rose a little larger than their base."

Descartes's brief descriptions go to the heart of both what's so obvious and so subtle about snowflakes. Every kid knows that

---

snowflakes are six-sided. But scientists still haven't solved the problem of how all snowflakes can be six-sided and yet take so many different shapes. If snowflakes are all made in roughly the same way, how is it that some are like "clockmaker's wheels" and others "crystal columns," miniature six-sided pillars? (Incidentally, Descartes was fortunate to see those columns capped on either end by a "six-petalled rose," like wheels attached to an axle — many veteran snowflake watchers see these only once or twice in a lifetime.)

What's amazing about Descartes's description is that it's apparently only the second time anyone in Europe acknowledged, in print, that all snowflakes are six-sided! The credit for first mention goes to Johannes Kepler, an astronomer known mostly for his work on the shapes of planetary orbits, who in 1611 wrote a little book called *The Six-Cornered Snowflake*. If you go back a half-century before that, it's apparent that the hexagonal shape of snowflakes was not common knowledge in Europe. A woodcut in a 1555 book by the Archbishop of Uppsala shows twenty-three versions of snowflakes, only one of which is six-sided. The variety of the other shapes depicted — eyes, hands, bells, arrows and half-moons — makes it clear that the author had no idea which shape was correct. In contrast, the Chinese had described the true shape of snowflakes at least as early as the second century A.D.

At first glance it seems ridiculous that four hundred years ago no one in Europe knew, or at least publicly acknowledged, that all snowflakes are six-sided. You usually don't have to spend more than a few moments in falling snow before you can find individual six-sided flakes on the windshield of your car or the sleeve of your coat. On the other hand, it's always easier to see something if you already know it exists — would we notice those perfect little hexagons so readily if we hadn't been taught from kindergarten that they're there?

Recognizing that snowflakes are six-sided is only the beginning — even Kepler realized that the really interesting question is why? What mould or force could produce millions of flakes out of frozen water that, whether flat plates or columns or stars, all have six sides? He figured that snowflakes must be assembled from smaller sub-units, and that six-sidedness had something to do with packing them together efficiently. He was intrigued by the fact that hexagons appeared in other situations where efficient packing was paramount, as in the individual cells in a bee's honeycomb, or even the arrangement of seeds in a pomegranate. But he couldn't explain why snowflakes are six-sided.

It wasn't until this century that at least part of Kepler's question could be answered. The architecture of snowflakes depends first on the water molecule itself. Water is, of course, two atoms of hydrogen and one of oxygen: H_2O. At room temperature, when water is liquid, the H_2O molecules are vibrating and sliding past each other, colliding and recoiling, leaving virtually no space between them. But if the temperature drops low enough, this normal jostling of water molecules relative to each other can be overcome by electrical forces acting among them, and they then all snap into fixed positions relative to each other. That's freezing.

When freezing immobilizes the water molecules, it forces them to move apart and take only rigid arms-length positions with respect to each other. X-rays of such ice crystals reveal a remarkable repeating pattern of hexagons: six water molecules at each corner, in turn bonded to other water molecules beside, above and below. Kepler was closer than he realized: at the micro level, a mass of ice crystals looks like a vast honeycomb.

This repeating hexagonal pattern holds the key to snowflakes. Under the right circumstances in the atmosphere, a crystal will start to grow (usually by latching onto a microscopic dust particle), adding water molecules to its edges, always preserving the underlying hexagonal organization. By the time it's big enough to see, you have a snowflake. [The rigidity and immobility that I've implied exists in an ice crystal is relatively true, when you compare it to liquid water, but such a crystal is by no means totally inactive. There's evidence that the average water molecule in an ice crystal jumps out of its position once every millionth of a second, wanders a little way down the crystal, maybe a distance of eight molecules or so, then kicks another H_2O out of its place, and jumps back into the crystal.]

The greatest snowflake scientist of the twentieth century is the late Ukichiro Nakaya, a nuclear physicist whose life was changed when he had the (mis)fortune to be appointed to a chair of physics in Hokkaido, the north island of Japan, in 1932. The university there didn't have the facilities to do nuclear physics, but they did have lots of snow. Nakaya took the pragmatic approach and changed his field of study. He was the first scientist to produce snowflakes in the lab. He strung rabbit hairs like miniature clotheslines in cold chambers filled with water vapour. Rabbit hairs are lined with little nodules that provide the same opportunity for initiating the growth of snowflakes as do dust particles in the air: snow crystals can settle on them and begin to add new crystals from the surrounding air.

Nakaya showed for the first time why snowflakes can be anything from delicate, feathery six-fingered stars to blunt six-sided shields, or even the pillars with hexagonal caps on both ends that Descartes mentioned. Their shapes reflect their histories — as Nakaya wrote: "a snowflake is a letter to us from the sky."

Temperature and humidity are the key — as they change, the way snow crystals grow changes as well. If a snowflake is forming in fairly dry air at −15 degrees Celsius, it will be plate-shaped, but at 10 degrees less than that it will form as a solid column. The feathery six-armed Christmas card snowflakes develop only in very wet air at around −14 degrees Celsius. You can imagine how complicated it can be if a snowflake starts at one temperature and humidity, then is carried by winds up, then down, first moving quickly, then slowly (differences in speed affect the growth of the crystal), then finally falling to earth, encountering yet more changes in temperature and humidity. With each change the growing flake will alter its ongoing pattern, while preserving what's already there. As Nakaya suggested, you could read the history of that flake by its shape.

Why should temperature and humidity make so much difference? If every ice crystal, at least at the molecular level, is exactly the same, why isn't every snowflake the same? This question is right at the frontiers of physics. Everyone agrees on the general picture: free-floating water molecules, or small groups of them frozen together, bump into the growing snowflake and lock into place. The higher the humidity, the more molecules competing for available spaces; the lower the temperature, the easier it is to form the solid bonds that hold them there. You can even imagine how a plate could change to a column — by growing up rather than out — and how a plate that grew only at its corners, rather than the edges, would soon grow arms. But it's nearly impossible to know what the exact conditions are in the microscopic neighbourhood of the crystal, and that's where tiny differences in temperature or numbers of water molecules might change one shape to another. The flakes that Descartes saw obviously started out as columns and suddenly changed to plates, yet these and almost all snowflakes end up perfectly symmetrical — you don't find them with one arm ten times longer than the others. But how does one end of a snowflake know to grow at just the right speed that it will balance what's happening on the other end? *That* may be the toughest question of all.

Finally, is it really true that there are no two snowflakes alike? Until 1988 the answer was yes; now it's yes . . . maybe. In May 1988, Nancy Knight of the National Center for Atmospheric Research in Boulder, Colorado, reported finding two snowflakes that were "virtually identical." These flakes were collected on November 1, 1986, by researchers studying clouds in an airplane flying at about 6,000 metres (20,000 feet). They're shaped like tiny columns with vase-shaped hollow centres, and appear to be the same. Mrs Knight, an experienced snow researcher, said it was the first time she had seen flakes like this, "which, if not identical, are certainly very much alike." Of course, it's impossible to know if these flakes were exactly identical — there's only one photo from one angle at one magnification. This leaves the door open for traditionalists to continue to rely on some very convincing statistics to argue that even these two probably weren't "identical."

Consider the number of snowflakes that have fallen on the earth since the beginning of the planet. One estimate is 10^{35} flakes of snow — that's 1 followed by 35 zeroes — a weight of snow fifty times the mass of the earth, even though each flake weighs only a millionth of a gram. Surely two of those would be the same? Well, you must take into account that each snowflake contains something like 10^{18} molecules of water, and those can be arranged in lots of different ways. What's lots? A rough calculation suggests that for an individual flake growing gradually as it falls, there might be a million occasions when water molecules have a choice of more than one place to attach. This makes the number of possible flakes incredibly huge, trillions of trillions of times greater than the total number of flakes that have ever fallen. Besides, how likely is it that two snowflakes would have exactly the same histories? Even two balloons released at exactly the same place at the same time travel different paths because of unpredictable breaths of air. And if that isn't enough, even snowflakes following exactly identical paths couldn't be the same, because the first one would absorb water molecules that then would be unavailable for the second.

The inescapable conclusion from the statistics is that it's overwhelmingly unlikely that any two snowflakes are identical. That being the case, where does Nancy Knight's photograph fit in? Either it's a picture of two flakes that are almost exactly the same, and so is a curiosity but not much more, or it really is the only existing record of two identical snowflakes. That would make that single photo a scientific masterpiece, the highlight of four hundred years of snowflake research.

RESPONSE

1. What do you think fascinated Descartes and Kepler about snowflakes?
2. In what ways is the structure of a snowflake "at the frontiers of physics"?
3. What do you think Nakaya meant when he referred to snowflakes as "letters from the sky"?

EXTENSION

4. In the resource centre, find answers to the following questions:
   a) What percentage of the earth's water is "fresh"?
   b) What percentage of this "fresh" water lies within Canada's boundaries?
   c) Trace the flow of North America's major watersheds.
5. For Debate: Canada should sell fresh water to the United States.
6. Write a reflective piece or poem on snow.

EARTHKEEPING

THE RUSSELL-EINSTEIN MANIFESTO

issued in London, July 9th 1955
BERTRAND RUSSELL and ALBERT EINSTEIN

- In groups, identify the five most serious problems which face humankind.
- As a class, examine the ways in which these problems are related.

I n the tragic situation which confronts humanity, we feel that scientists should assemble in conference to appraise the perils that have arisen as a result of the development of weapons of mass destruction, and to discuss a resolution in the spirit of the appended draft.

We are speaking on this occasion, not as members of this or that nation, continent, or creed, but as human beings, members of the species Man, whose continued existence is in doubt. The world is full of conflicts; and, overshadowing all minor conflicts, the titanic struggle between Communism and anti-Communism.

Almost everybody who is politically conscious has strong feelings about one or more of these issues; but we want you, if you can, to set aside such feelings and consider yourselves only as members of a biological species which has had a remarkable history, and whose disappearance none of us can desire.

We shall try to say no single word which should appeal to one group rather than to another. All, equally, are in peril, and, if the peril is understood, there is hope that they may collectively avert it.

We have to learn to think in a new way. We have to learn to ask ourselves, not what steps can be taken to give military victory to whatever group we prefer, for there no longer are such steps; the question we have to ask ourselves is: what steps can be taken to prevent a military contest of which the issue must be disastrous to all parties?

The general public, and even many men in positions of authority, have not realized what would be involved in a war with nuclear bombs. The general public still thinks in terms of the obliteration of cities. It is understood that the new bombs are more powerful than the old, and that, while one A-bomb could obliterate Hiroshima, one H-bomb could obliterate the largest cities, such as London, New York, and Moscow.

No doubt in an H-bomb war great cities would be obliterated. But this is one of the minor disasters that would have to be faced. If everybody in London, New York, and Moscow were exterminated, the world might, in the course of a few centuries, recover from the blow. But we now know, especially since the Bikini test, that nuclear bombs can gradually spread destruction over a very much wider area than had been supposed.

It is stated on very good authority that a bomb can now be manufactured which will be 2,500 times as powerful as that which destroyed Hiroshima. Such a bomb, if exploded near the ground or under water, sends radio-active particles into the upper air. They sink gradually and reach the surface of the earth in the form of a deadly dust or rain. It was this dust which infected the Japanese fishermen and their catch of fish.

No one knows how widely such lethal radio-active particles might be diffused, but the best authorities are unanimous in saying that a war with H-bombs might possibly put an end to the human race. It is feared that if many H-bombs are used there will be universal death — sudden only for a minority, but for the majority a slow torture of disease and disintegration.

Many warnings have been uttered by eminent men of science and by authorities in military strategy. None of them will say that the worst results are certain. What they do say is that these results are possible, and no one can be sure that they will not be realized. We have not yet found that the views of experts on this question depend in any degree upon their politics or prejudices. They depend only, so far as our researches have revealed, upon the extent of the particular expert's knowledge. We have found that the men who know most are the most gloomy.

Here, then, is the problem which we present to you, stark and dreadful and inescapable: Shall we put an end to the human race; or shall mankind renounce war? People will not face this alternative because it is so difficult to abolish war.

The abolition of war will demand distasteful limitations of national sovereignty. But what perhaps impedes understanding of the situation more than anything else is that the term "mankind" feels vague and abstract. People scarcely realize in imagination that the danger is to themselves and their children and their grandchildren, and not only to a dimly apprehended humanity. They can scarcely bring themselves to grasp that they, individually, and those whom they love are in imminent danger of perishing agonizingly. And so they hope that perhaps war may be allowed to continue provided modern weapons are prohibited.

This hope is illusory. Whatever agreements not to use H-bombs had been reached in time of peace, they would no longer be considered binding in time of war, and both sides would set to work to manufacture H-bombs as soon as war broke out, for, if one side manufactured the bombs and the other did not, the side that manufactured them would inevitably be victorious.

Although an agreement to renounce nuclear weapons as part of a general reduction of armaments would not afford an ultimate solution, it would serve certain important purposes. First: any agreement between East and West is to the good in so far as it tends to diminish tension. Second: the abolition of thermo-nuclear weapons, if each side believed that the other had carried it out sincerely, would lessen the fear of a sudden attack in the style of Pearl Harbour, which at present keeps both sides in a state of nervous apprehension. We should, therefore, welcome such an agreement, though only as a first step.

Most of us are not neutral in feeling, but, as human beings, we have to remember that, if the issues between East and West are to be decided in any manner that can give any possible satisfaction to anybody, whether Communist or anti-Communist, whether

Asian or European or American, whether White or Black, then these issues must not be decided by war. We should wish this to be understood, both in the East and in the West.

There lies before us, if we choose, continual progress in happiness, knowledge, and wisdom. Shall we, instead, choose death, because we cannot forget our quarrels? We appeal, as human beings, to human beings: Remember your humanity, and forget the rest. If you can do so, the way lies open to a new Paradise; if you cannot, there lies before you the risk of universal death.

Resolution
We invite this Congress, and through it the scientists of the world and the general public, to subscribe to the following resolution:

"In view of the fact that in any future world war nuclear weapons will certainly be employed, and that such weapons threaten the continued existence of mankind, we urge the Governments of the world to realize, and to acknowledge publicly, that their purpose cannot be furthered by a world war, and we urge them, consequently, to find peaceful means for the settlement of all matters of dispute between them."

MAX BORN
PEREY W. BRIDGMAN
ALBERT EINSTEIN
LEOPOLD INFELD
FREDERIC JOLIOT-CURIE
HERMAN J. MULLER
LINUS PAULING
CECIL F. POWELL
JOSEPH ROTBLAT
BERTRAND RUSSELL
HIDEKI YUKAWA

RESPONSE

1. "We have to learn to think in a new way."
   a) What does this mean for humankind?
   b) How can *you* think in a new way?
2. "Remember your humanity, and forget the rest." What do you think Russell and Einstein mean you to take from this?

3. In groups, write a manifesto for your English classroom which will help you think and act in new ways.
4. In your journal, write a personal manifesto.

PLAYING RUSSIAN ROULETTE WITH WORLD ENVIRONMENT

DAVID SUZUKI

- Recount a story you may have heard about your local environment which describes it as it was some time ago.
- What do you think should be the nature of the relationship between humankind and the environment?

In the mid-fifties, while I was returning from college in the United States for the summer, I glanced down at the Niagara River as my train passed over. Below, I could see fishermen on the banks flailing away at the water and yanking silver objects from the river as fast as they could cast. They were catching silver bass on a massive annual spawning run.

Those spring runs petered out years ago.

Old fishermen on the east and west coasts of Canada describe an abundance and size of salmon, cod and lobsters when they were starting out that younger fishermen have never seen. It wasn't long ago that we drank from the Great Lakes with confidence in the water's purity, and relished fresh fruits and vegetables without concern about chemical contamination. Only a few decades ago, the quality of our water, soil and air was radically different and there were an abundance and variety of life that now are found only in the most remote parts of the country.

The planet has changed almost beyond recognition within the life-time of Canada's elder citizens. Their recollections are not simply old folks' romantic musings on the good old days; they are a living record of the cataclysmic degradation that has taken place around us. In the past, men took canaries into coal mines as biological indicators of the quality of the air; today, our elders are the ones who know that canaries are falling all around us.

Our species boasts the highest ratio of "brain to brawn"of all life forms, and that mental power has gifted us with a conscious strategy for survival. We have invented a notion called the "future," which provided us with options and enabled us to deliberately select a future toward which we aimed. Yet today, with all the amplified brainpower of computers, communications networks, scientists and engineers, we seem unable to use the strategy that got our forebears to where we took over. What has gone wrong?

I believe that we continue to cling to certain "sacred truths" that blind us to many problems and often cause the ones that we do recognize. Let me list some of those sacred truths.
• We equate "progress" with *growth* — growth in the economy, income, consumer goods, material comfort. A need for steady economic growth is repeated like a catechism by every politician, economist and businessperson, and has led us to link *profit* with the goal of society. But human beings today are the most ubiquitous and numerous large mammal in the world, and it is our unrelenting commitment to growth that now has us consuming 40 per cent of the net primary production of energy on the planet. We are only one species among perhaps 30 million. When our population doubles again within 50 years, will we then demand 80 per cent? Nothing on this planet continues indefinitely to grow steadily.

The current increases in consumption and material wealth are a historical aberration, a blip that will come to a stop within our children's lifetime. The only question is whether we will deliberately bring our demands and consumption under control or allow pestilence, famine or war to do the job.

• We have come to believe in the ability of science to provide us with the knowledge to understand and manage our natural resources. Yet the unique power of science is that its practitioners focus on an isolated part of nature, and thus increase knowledge in fragmented bits and pieces. Modern physicists have learned that it is not possible to put these fragments of knowledge together into a complete picture, because in real life, unlike a jigsaw puzzle, the pieces interact synergistically. Thus, properties emerge from the complex that cannot be anticipated from the known properties of the component parts.

As a result, there are fundamental reasons why it is not possible to comprehend the behavior of entire ecosystems or even complex components within them. In addition, the degree of our ignorance remains vast. We know very little, for example, about chinook salmon during their four-year stay in the ocean, yet we maintain the illusion that we are managing them scientifically.

• We believe we can manage the effects of new technologies by doing proper cost/benefit analysis to maximize the benefits while minimizing costs. History informs us that every technology, however beneficial, has costs. And invariably the benefits of new technologies are immediate and obvious. That's why we (including me) love technology; it does such wonderful things for us. But the costs of these technologies are almost always hidden, and cannot be anticipated.

If all technologies exact a price that cannot be foreseen, can we continue to mortgage the future by opting for the immediate benefits of new inventions while postponing the solution to their accompanying costs? Today scientists speak of building machines that can think, tampering with the heredity of babies, manipulating the human mind and releasing genetically engineered organisms into the environment — yet we cannot predict their long-term consequences.

• We believe we can minimize environmental damage from our activity by carrying out environmental assessments. Thus, for example, oil exploration in the high Arctic or off Georges Bank or building a fixed link to Prince Edward Island, depend on the success of an environmental assessment review process (EARP). Of course, there should be such assessments, but in view of how little we know of the constituents of ecosystems and their interactions, fluctuations over time and the tiny window our tests provide, the EARP is far too limited in scope, duration and scale to provide information that is statistically meaningful.

We cannot assume that once an EARP indicates no hazard, development should have an unconditional green light. Approval should always be provisional, with a continued accumulation of information on which reassessments of that approval are constantly made.

• We believe that in a democracy, we elect people to political office to represent and lead us into the future. Yet most politicians come from two professions, business and law, the two areas whose practitioners have the poorest comprehension of issues scientific and technological.

Today, the most important factor shaping our lives and society is science when applied by industry, medicine and the military. Yet, jurisdictional concerns such as Meech Lake and economic priorities of free trade preoccupy our leaders and subsume the priorities of the planet's ecosystem.

"Conventional wisdom" assumes the truth of the above assumptions. Unless we expose them to the light of critical examination, we will continue to ravage the ecosystem for short-term benefits. We desperately need a new paradigm, a new vision of the human place in nature.

We live in a time when satellites have sent back images of this planet that graphically demonstrate its oneness. I think ecologist Jack Vallentyne, who poses as Johnny Biosphere to instruct children about the environment, is on the right track. He reminds us that we all have built into our cells and tissues, atoms and molecules that were once in the bodies of all other people on the planet and of people who lived one or two thousand years ago. Not only that, but we are made of atoms respired by trees and insects and mammals and birds. That's because all life forms share the atmosphere around the world.

Johnny Biosphere tells of an Indian who, on a hot day hundreds of years ago, swam in Lake Superior. Sodium ions from the sweat of his body are still contained in each drink of water that we take from Lake Ontario. And when one realizes that everything we eat for nutrition was itself once living, we realize that we remain inextricably linked to the rest of life on this planet. Seen in this perspective of sharing and connectedness, we have to behave in a radically different way when we dispose of our wastes or apply new technologies that affect other parts of the ecosystem.

Throughout human history, the boast of our species has been that we love our children and hope that they will have a richer, fuller life than we did. Yet now, for the first time, we know with absolute certainty that our children's lives will be immeasurably poorer in bio-diversity and filled with massive problems that we have foisted on them in our shortsighted pursuit of immediate profit and power.

Can we continue to mortgage our children's future so thoughtlessly? Not if we mean it when we say we love them.

RESPONSE

1. In your group, determine which of the "sacred truths" is most destructive to the environment.
2. a) What are you doing now that will have a negative effect on the lives of any children you may have?
   b) What are you doing now that will have a positive effect on those same children's lives?

EXTENSION

3. What are the "sacred truths" in your school/home/community that are harmful and must be changed?
4. Devise a plan to change the impact of those "sacred truths."

HAUT VERT

EVE DROBOT

- Are there people you know who refuse to take any action to benefit the environment? Explain.
- What changes have you noticed in your community which will benefit the environment?

"Okay, that's tea sandwiches for fifty, scones, Devonshire cream," said the caterer. "And, of course, you'll want rental plates. The paper ones are so unecological."

"Green" is this year's colour. Everyone is trying to look good in it. Hostesses send out invitations on obviously recycled paper. Gardening club members boast about the size of their compost heaps. About 175,000 copies (and still counting) of *The Canadian Green Consumer Guide* have sold so far, and some of those books went to very good homes. Green can be extremely profitable, as the Loblaws supermarket chain has discovered with its highly successful pro-environment retooling of products. Green can be beautiful if you swear off overly packaged cosmetics that have been tested on animals and buy your balms and unguents at The Body Shop, which certifies the organic and political purity of its products. Green can be chic if you go shopping carrying a Provençal straw basket and forsake plastic bags. Green can be the height of luxury if you buy your baubles at Birks, which has banned all African ivory from its velvet display cases.

Parliament Hill is turning green, under the aegis of the Speaker of the House of Commons, John Fraser. Recycling is high on his personal order paper, which, according to his assistant, Jim Watson, is "to turn the Commons into an environmental showcase for all government buildings." That MPs' seats in the Commons are upholstered green is a coincidence, but the blue baskets for recycling paper are not. The print shop tries to double-side all photocopies; halls and offices are lit with energy-efficient light bulbs; Styrofoam cups have been banned from offices and meeting rooms; one House of Commons vehicle has been converted to propane and another to natural gas; and all and sundry have been kindly requested to snitch on any ministerial car caught idling at the front door.

No one will dispute that "green is good," but a few folks are muttering that it's taking its toll on their nerves. Writer Amy Willard Cross complained in *The Globe and Mail* that she has become an "enviro-neurotic" who can't turn on a light without worrying about "coal-burning plants, sulphuric acid, northern fish and trees dying of acid rain." The cafeteria at that newspaper has been up and down on the ecological seesaw with staff who first complained about food served on paper plates, then neglected to return china plates to be washed, forcing the cafeteria to bring in disposables again, causing the staff to complain about the paper plates and . . .

Families are feeling the pressure, especially in righteous Toronto. One well-heeled executive worries that he and his wife will have "the world's first ecological divorce." His wastrel ways are testing her environmental mettle, and the couple who maintain they never argue are now yelling at each other over whether to take the car or public transit. A mother recounts with a combination of public humiliation and pride how her teenage daughter marches into McDonald's and orders "a Big Mac, hold the Styrofoam box."

The green-willed can't win for losing sometimes. A politically correct doctor caught standing at a cheese counter at the St. Lawrence market laden down with plastic shopping bags feels honour-bound to justify himself: "I'd like to carry a canvas tote, but we need the plastic bags for the garbage cans. If I don't bring the groceries home in plastic bags, we'd have to go out and *buy* garbage bags and encourage the manufacturers to go on producing them. I can't decide which is worse."

And an impeccable, elegant matron buys herself a lovely fur coat and feels at peace with herself and her four-legged friends because it is fake. But it is of such high quality that it doesn't look fake. And therein lies the rub. Will the anti-fur militants rumoured to be trolling the fashionable avenues know not to splatter her with fake blood? Not to worry. The coat's manufacturer proudly provides her with a guarantee: he has affixed a brass badge on the pocket she can flash at would-be attackers declaring the coat to be the ersatz it really is. Moral mace. So all's right with the world. Or is it? A few months after her purchase, a friend takes her to task for buying an article of clothing made from petroleum by-products, unbiodegradable in the extreme. As Kermit the Frog once pointed out, "It's not easy being green."

RESPONSE

1. Do you think that "consumer awareness" is a fad or a genuine desire to do less harm to the environment? Explain.
2. What do you think Amy Willard Cross means when she describes herself as an "enviro-neurotic"?
3. What environmentally related choices do you find most difficult to make?

EXTENSION

4. What obstacles do you have to overcome to improve the quality of your environment?
5. In your group, develop a strategy to overcome these obstacles.

TREASURES OF THE SIERRA MADRE

CHRISTIE McLAREN

- Find out how migratory birds navigate.
- Write a short piece about some aspect of the natural world that interests you.

A t first, all Toby Clark could see was the fungus. Deep, furry fungus. But then, it was difficult to see much of anything, stumbling around in the dark. Clark — a Washington economist on a Mexican vacation — was still half asleep. He had forced himself awake, driven for hours on dirt roads, and now he was climbing on foot through the forest on a steep mountainside in the dark. All because he wanted to see a butterfly.

"As you got closer," Clark recalls, "all you could see was . . . a very heavy fungus growing on the trees and on the twigs and on the branches — a black fungus." But as the darkness slowly lifted, he began to see that the plush folds of fungus were, in fact, wings — millions of black-edged monarch butterfly wings folded in thick furrows on the bark and the branches.

"As the sun came over the tops of the mountains, it would begin shining into these trees — into big clumps of fungus — and suddenly," he says, "you'd see the wings move. And then with a silent *poof*, a clump would explode. You watched it, all these

butterflies flying up from this clump. And these clumps would
continue exploding as they got warmed up, until the air was filled
with hundreds of thousands, or maybe millions, of butterflies.
And very slowly, they were just circling. They weren't going
anywhere. The whole sky and everything around you was filled
with these butterflies, and if you stood there quietly, they'd land
all over you."

For two silent hours Clark stood there, watching clump after
clump of semi-dormant butterflies erupt into soft, slow explo-
sions, filling the air with lazy flecks of orange and black, until the
sun was high in the sky. "It was one of the most wondrous sights
I've ever seen," he says with unselfconscious awe. "I compare it
to the first time I saw the Taj Mahal in moonlight. It was a
completely wondrous sight in terms of sheer beauty."

The majesty of the monarch butterfly has long been known to
the Mazahuas people of central Mexico, who have aptly named the
large insects "daughters of the sun." But although monarchs have
been around for more than 50 million years, and generations of
Mexicans knew where they wintered, the rest of the world did not
learn their secret until 1975. It took a remarkable discovery led by
a Canadian scientist to prove that the monarch is also king of the
migrating insects.

For Canadian zoologist Fred Urquhart, the discovery of the
monarchs' Mexican hideaway was the fulfillment of a dream, and
the end of a 40-year mystery. It was in 1937 that Urquhart, a
University of Toronto zoologist, and his wife, Norah, first became
obsessed with the biological detective story that was to absorb
them for the next four decades. They — and a host of other
scientists and naturalists — knew that when autumn arrived, the
monarchs of eastern North America vanished south. But where
exactly did they go?

The answer depended on tracking the butterflies. But butterflies
are not birds, and tagging them proved difficult. The Urquharts
tried labels and liquid glue. They tried pre-pasted postage-stamp
stickers. After several years and many failures, they finally found
a label that stuck: tiny gummed price tags, applied with a squeeze
to a section of butterfly wing where the scales had been removed,
would stay on even under water.

Each label bore letters and numbers identifying where the
insects were tagged, as well as the instruction: "Send to Zoology

University Toronto Canada." After Urquhart appealed to amateur naturalists through a magazine article in 1952, 12 volunteers came forward. By 1971, 600 people across eastern North America were involved in the search. By 1976, hundreds of thousands of people from Maine to California had mailed butterflies or tags to Toronto.

Fuelled by volunteer donations and research grants from the National Geographic Society and the National Research Council of Canada, the Urquharts began field work in 1965 that enabled them to rule out Florida and the Gulf Coast as monarch destinations. Meanwhile, the trickle of tagged butterflies turned into a pattern that they plotted on a large wall chart. To the Urquharts' surprise, it seemed the monarchs were flying diagonally across the continent, from northeast to southwest, through Texas to Mexico. "We never suspected that they went to Mexico — not by a long shot," Dr. Urquhart said in a recent interview. "But that's where they went."

In 1972, Norah Urquhart wrote a series of letters to Mexican newspapers. The following February, an amateur naturalist named Kenneth Brugger wrote back with an offer of help. Brugger's regular drives through the countryside paid off in April 1974, when he reported seeing many monarchs flying at random in the Sierra Madre area of central Mexico. Later that year, he found roads littered with dead and tattered butterflies. On January 9, 1975 the Urquharts received a long-distance telephone call. Brugger had found millions of monarchs huddled together in the trees near a mountain clearing.

The news set the science world agog. But it wasn't until a year later — one year to the day — that Fred and Norah Urquhart first saw the butterflies for themselves. "It's such an emotional thing .... You'd have to go and see it. You can't really explain it," Urquhart insists today. "After all that work, being able to suddenly look at it . . . was like a gift from the gods. No one will ever compete with me and my wife on that one, on emotion."

Deepening the scientists' emotion, of course, was their knowledge that the butterflies had conquered incredible odds to reach Mexico. Each had journeyed up to 4000 kilometres, travelling unerringly from scattered points in southern Canada and the eastern United States, to reach this tiny dot on the map.

How does this insect — a fragile, featherweight, jewel-like scrap of membrane and protein — do it? Straight out of a textbook theory of creativity, the answer came from a scientist's daydream.

One late summer day in 1977 another U. of T. zoologist, David Gibo, was gazing absently out his fourth-floor office window on the university's Mississauga campus, thinking about flying his glider plane, when a monarch fluttered into view. As it neared the vertical wall of the building, he noticed that the butterfly stopped flapping its wings. "Suddenly," he says, "it just gained altitude," and floated effortlessly up and out of sight.

An experienced glider pilot, Gibo knew instantly that the butterfly was exploiting a principle of aerodynamics used to advantage by eagles, seagulls and gliders. It was "soaring" on an upward draft of air that formed as the wind hit the vertical wall of the building — the same kind of updraft that forms around mountains and canyons. Gibo began to study the butterflies and found that, like glider planes, they also ride "thermals," columns of warm, upward-rising air that form when the air near the ground heats up, becomes lighter than the air above it, and starts to rise.

Using thermals to propel them up and forward, the monarchs literally ride the winds to Mexico, soaring as high as 2134 metres above the ground. At this height, Gibo has calculated, the average half-gram butterfly with a ten-centimetre wing span could glide an incredible five kilometres before being forced to flap for power again. It travels this way for six or seven hours a day, at an average speed of 12.8 kilometres an hour, covering about 65 kilometres and sometimes even 100 kilometres before stopping for the night. Scientists think the butterflies rarely fly in the dark unless they are over water and cannot land.

All this has earned the monarch the distinction of having the "furthest directional migration of any insect," Gibo says. Locusts, while long-distance travellers too, merely ride weather systems wherever they go. By contrast, Gibo says, "the butterflies have a goal — and they'll get there whatever the winds are. They're a tough insect."

To get there in the quickest way possible, the monarchs have choreographed at least 20 different manoeuvres to cope with uncooperative winds. Flying southwest, they manoeuvre to avoid downdrafts and, when a thermal dies, just flap their wings to find another. When the wind changes, blowing from the southeast toward the northwest, they head into it much the same way a sailboat "tacks," allowing the wind to propel them west while at the same time staying close to the ground and flapping their wings to get themselves south. Curiously, Gibo says, when the wind is blowing toward the southeast, the butterflies don't fight it, allowing themselves to be blown far off course toward Florida or the Atlantic Ocean. Why? Under pressure to flee the fast-approaching cold weather, he theorizes, the monarchs will hitch a ride on the wrong wind east as long as it is also heading south.

Soaring in this fashion, the monarchs use less than 1 percent of the energy it would take to flap their wings for the same distance, Gibo says. This may help to explain why butterflies arrive in Mexico five times fatter than when they left. That extra fat will be used to help them survive during hibernation in the near-zero temperatures and to fuel the flight back north in the spring.

At least one other characteristic helps millions of monarchs survive the migration — their nasty taste. Many birds avoid the monarch, despite its appealing colours, because it contains a heart poison that is fatal to most vertebrates. This deadly potion is manufactured when the monarch digests its main food, milkweed.

The butterflies' flight — or float — to the south is all the more astonishing because none of them has ever done it before. Gibo and other scientists are now avidly probing the greatest remaining mystery surrounding the migration. They are trying to learn how the monarch steers.

It's a simple thing. It is also arguably the most complex. On the surface, the butterflies appear to have a guidance system that rivals that of the Cruise missile. "The classic view," says Gibo, "is that they are complicated computer programs."

Every nervous system, even a butterfly's, produces its own unique energy field through electro-chemical reactions in the body's cells. Each electrical field is altered slightly as it travels through a magnetic field, like that produced by the earth. Every position on earth, in turn, has a different angle of magnetic inclination. Recent studies by European scientists have found that monarch butterflies flying over two different geographic regions of the United States flew consistently in slightly different directions — directions predicted by a mathematical formula based on the earth's magnetic inclination. But this pattern only works until the insects hit Georgia, Gibo says. Then they turn west and it falls apart.

So that is only part of the puzzle. For the missing pieces, Gibo and other scientists are turning back to the sun. They speculate that like birds, bees, ants and ancient civilizations, the butterflies could be using the sun for a compass. Its position in the sky may tell the insects where to fly.

A third, more controversial theory says the monarch has a natural built-in compass. A few years ago Gibo and another scientist analyzed the butterflies to see if their bodies contained "magnetite" — a magnetic material that would allow them to use the earth's magnetic field as a guide. But after one promising experiment and several that produced no magnetite, Gibo now concludes "there's no evidence for it." Indeed, he cautions that each theory of butterfly navigation is just that, as few studies have been done and there is no proof. With the aid of grants from the National Science and Engineering Council, however, Gibo says he is among a small number of scientists who are trying to unravel the monarch's flight strategies.

After making their complicated way to Mexico by mid-November, the monarchs sleep until mid-March in the oyamel forests about three hours' drive north of Mexico City. As the days begin to lengthen, scientists theorize, something about the light or angle of the sun stirs them awake, and they mate and depart on their return migration.

They lay their eggs on the underside of milkweed leaves in northern Mexico or Texas, and the nine-month life cycle of this lepidopterous insect, *Danaus plexippus linnaeus*, begins. A black, white and yellow-striped caterpillar emerges from each egg three to 12 days later and immediately starts feeding on milkweed. More than two weeks later, after growing and shedding several skins, the larva finds a sheltered spot, weaves a thick web of silk and sheds its last skin to reveal the sea-green gold-spotted pupa. About two weeks later, this pouch turns transparent, exposing the markings of a grown butterfly. The chrysalis wall soon cracks and the limp wings emerge to stretch and dry their scales.

The five-week cycle from egg to butterfly is repeated about four times before September as the butterflies move north. As a result, different generations of butterflies enter Canada and the northern United States in late May and June. Observers have noticed tattered, faded butterflies and bright new ones. But there is no proof that any monarchs that started out in Mexico are able to complete the full journey back to Canada.

In late August or early September, the fourth, migratory generation emerges. Unlike the others, it does not mature sexually. It is these butterflies, their energy unspent by mating, that embark on the long journey south, which is triggered by the shorter, cooler days. Flying by the millions, but without flocking together, they reach central Mexico by mid-November, two-and-a-half months later, after feeding in the southern U.S. on milkweed and wildflowers such as aster and sunflower.

A small proportion of butterflies from west of the Rockies winter on the southern California coast. With so many warm southern destinations like these to choose from, scientists are still not sure why the majority of monarchs head for Mexico.

Dr. Urquhart believes the butterflies may be returning to their primordial roost. "Because more than half of North America's 100 species of milkweed are native to Mexico, a tempting hypothesis arises. May it not be that, far back in geologic time, the monarch originated in Mexico? Now, in returning there each winter, the butterfly is 'going home' after straying, perhaps over eras of a warming trend, farther and ever farther north."

Another theory has it that the near-freezing temperatures and the shelter of the Sierra Madre forests provide the perfect winter habitat, allowing the insects to sink into semi-hibernation and conserve valuable energy without freezing.

Whatever the reason, the discovery that the monarchs winter in the neo-volcanic axis of central Mexico at 2,740 metres started a seven-year international campaign — inspired by Urquhart and fuelled by some influential butterfly fans in Mexico — to save the oyamel forests.

The dynamic leader of the environmental crusade in Mexico City was Rodolfo Ogarrio, a Harvard-trained lawyer and close school chum of Brian Dickson, chief justice of the Supreme Court of Canada. In 1980, Ogarrio helped to found Monarca A.C., a non-profit organization established to protect the butterfly.

That March, the Mexican government issued a decree to protect the monarch, including a closed season on hunting in the area. But it did little good since the land itself remained unprotected. Local farmers who were gradually clearing the high fir forest for farmland and timber still posed a grave threat to the butterflies' sanctuaries. Although Mexican federal and state governments were willing to expropriate or buy small portions of the area that needed protection, vast areas remained in jeopardy.

But Ogarrio can be very persuasive, and eventually, after what Urquhart calls "a terrible fight," a solution was hatched.

"I said to Ogarrio: 'what we've got to do is make this profitable for the people,' " Urquhart recalls. Monarca and World Wildlife Fund, which has donated more than $200,000 since 1976 to monarch research and Monarca, set out to create an alternate source of income for the local residents.

Tourism was the most logical substitute. Hotels could fill up with butterfly fans: local residents could become tour guides; and the people could do a brisk business making and selling pottery, decals and T-shirts to tourists. They have. And in the end, they convinced everyone that the monarchs can make money. "Now," Urquhart says with evident relish, "the people are saying: 'If you touch one of those monarchs, we'll kill you.'"

In August, 1986 the Mexican government established the "Ecological Reserve for the Protection of the Monarch Butterfly." It consists of 16 100 hectares spread over six separate areas in the central states of Mexico and Michoacan. They include "core" zones totalling 4490 hectares, where logging is prohibited and research is the only human activity allowed: and "buffer" zones totalling 11 619 hectares where logging is temporarily banned, but "economically productive activities" may be condoned by SEDUE, the Secretariat of Urban Development and Ecology. Meanwhile, the government has the areas under guard and is promoting tourism.

Last August 22, the reserve was formally dedicated in a ceremony attended by a host of dignitaries, Canadian and Mexican. But the man who made it all possible could not attend. Fred Urquhart was in a Toronto hospital that day undergoing open-heart surgery. But he was not forgotten. While many key aspects of the monarch migration remain a mystery, what is clear is that Dr. Urquhart's pioneering work has been crucial to the butterfly's survival.

"The world owes him a tremendous debt," says Iola Price, who attended the dedication as co-ordinator of Latin American programs for the Canadian Wildlife Service. "It's he that raised the public profile of the monarch to such heights. If he hadn't gone to all that work of tagging those butterflies, it could have taken forever."

Urquhart, meanwhile, says he cannot handle the flood of requests for interviews about his story. The continuing interest in the monarch appears to baffle and delight him. "It's amazing to me," he said. "I never thought it would reach this extreme. But everybody seems to love this little butterfly."

RESPONSE

1. Why did Fred and Norah Urquhart spend *four decades* tracking the flight and ultimate destination of the monarch butterfly?
2. What features of the monarch butterfly do you find most interesting?
3. What strategies did the Mexican government devise to protect the habitat of the monarch?

EXTENSION

4. With your group, investigate the bird and butterfly migratory patterns in your region. Report your findings to the class.
5. Enlist the aid of a science teacher to help you conduct a short "transit" of a green area around your school, such as a playing field or a park.

SOJOURNERS

ANNIE DILLARD

- What is your favourite tree? Explain.
- In a group, make a list of the tree products you use.

I
f survival is an art, then mangroves are artists of the beautiful:
not only that they exist at all — smooth-barked, glossy-leaved,
thickets of lapped mystery — but that they can and do exist as
floating islands, as trees upright and loose, alive and homeless
on the water.

I have seen mangroves, always on tropical ocean shores, in
Florida and in the Galàpagos. There is the red mangrove, the
yellow, the button, and the black. They are all short, messy trees,
waxy-leaved, laced all over with aerial roots, woody arching
buttresses, and weird leathery berry pods. All this tangles from a
black muck soil, a black muck matted like a mud-sopped rag, a
muck without any other plants, shaded, cold to the touch, tracked
at the water's edge by herons and nosed by sharks.

It is these shoreline trees which, by a fairly common accident,
can become floating islands. A hurricane flood or a riptide can
wrest a tree from the shore, or from the mouth of a tidal river, and
hurl it into the ocean. It floats. It is a mangrove island, blown.

There are floating islands on the planet; it amazes me.
Credulous Pliny described some islands thought to be mangrove
islands floating on a river. The people called these river islands
the dancers, "because in any consort of musicians singing, they
stir and move at the stroke of the feet, keeping time and
measure."

Trees floating on rivers are less amazing than trees floating on
the poisonous sea. A tree cannot live in salt. Mangrove trees
exude salt from their leaves; you can see it, even on shoreline

black mangroves, as a thin white crust. Lick a leaf and your tongue curls and coils; your mouth's a heap of salt.

Nor can a tree live without soil. A hurricane-born mangrove island may bring its own soil to the sea. But other mangrove trees make their own soil — and their own islands — from scratch. These are the ones which interest me. The seeds germinate in the fruit on the tree. The germinated embryo can drop anywhere — say, onto a dab of floating muck. The heavy root end sinks; a leafy plumule unfurls. The tiny seedling, afloat, is on its way. Soon aerial roots shooting out in all directions trap debris. The sapling's networks twine, the interstices narrow, and water calms in the lee. Bacteria thrive on organic broth; amphipods swarm. These creatures grow and die at the trees' wet feet. The soil thickens, accumulating rainwater, leaf rot, seashells, and guano; the island spreads.

More seeds and more muck yield more trees on the new island. A society grows, interlocked in a tangle of dependencies. The island rocks less in the swells. Fish throng to the backwaters stilled in snarled roots. Soon, Asian mudskippers — little four-inch fish — clamber up the mangrove roots into the air and peer about from periscope eyes on stalks, like snails. Oysters clamp to submerged roots, as do starfish, dog whelk, and the creatures that live among tangled kelp. Shrimp seek shelter there, limpets a holdfast, pelagic birds a rest.

And the mangrove island wanders on, afloat and adrift. It walks teetering and wanton before the wind. Its fate and direction are random. It may bob across an ocean and catch on another mainland's shores. It may starve or dry while it is still a sapling. It may topple in a storm, or pitchpole. By the rarest of chances, it may stave into another mangrove island in a crash of clacking roots, and mesh. What it is most likely to do is drift anywhere in the alien ocean, feeding on death and growing, netting a makeshift soil as it goes, shrimp in its toes and terns in its hair.

We could do worse.

I alternate between thinking of the planet as home — dear and familiar stone hearth and garden — and as a hard land of exile in which we are all sojourners. Today I favour the latter view. The word "sojourner" occurs often in the English Old Testament. It invokes a nomadic people's sense of vagrancy, a praying people's knowledge of estrangement, a thinking people's intuition of sharp loss: "For we are strangers before thee, and sojourners, as were all our fathers: our days on the earth are as a shadow, and there is none abiding."

We don't know where we belong, but in times of sorrow it doesn't seem to be here, here with these silly pansies and witless mountains, here with sponges and hard-eyed birds. In times of sorrow the innocence of other creatures — from whom and with whom we evolved — seems a mockery. Their ways are not our ways. We seem set among them as among lifelike props for a tragedy — or a broad lampoon — on a thrust rock stage.

It doesn't seem to be here that we belong, here where space is curved, the earth is round, we're all going to die, and it seems as wise to stay in bed as budge. It is strange here, not quite warm enough, or too warm, too leafy, or inedible, or windy, or dead. It is not, frankly, the sort of home for people one would have thought of — although I lack the fancy to imagine another.

The planet itself is a sojourner in airless space, a wet ball flung across nowhere. The few objects in the universe scatter. The coherence of matter dwindles and crumbles toward stillness. I have read, and repeated, that our solar system as a whole is careering through space toward a point east of Hercules. Now I wonder: what could that possibly mean, east of Hercules? Isn't space curved? When we get "there" how will our course change and why? Will we slide down the universe's inside arc like mud slung at a wall? Or what sort of welcoming shore is this east of Hercules? Surely we don't anchor there, and disembark, and sweep into dinner with our host. Does someone cry, "Last stop, last stop"? At any rate, east of Hercules, like east of Eden, isn't a place to call home. It is a course without direction; it is "out." And we are cast.

These are enervating thoughts, the thoughts of despair. They crowd back, unbidden, when human life as it unrolls goes ill, when we lose control of our lives or the illusion of control, and it seems that we are not moving toward any end but merely blown. Our life seems cursed to be a wiggle merely, and a wandering without end. Even nature is hostile and poisonous, as though it were impossible for our vulnerability to survive on these acrid stones.

Whether these thoughts are true or not I find less interesting than the possibilities for beauty they may hold. We are down here in time, where beauty grows. Even if things are as bad as they could possibly be, and as meaningless, then matters of truth are themselves indifferent; we may as well please our sensibilities and, with as much spirit as we can muster, go out with a buck and wing.

The planet is less like an enclosed spaceship — spaceship earth — than it is like an exposed mangrove island beautiful and loose. We the people started small and have since accumulated a great and solacing muck of soil, of human culture. We are rooted in it; we are bearing it with us across nowhere. The word "nowhere" is our cue: the consort of musicians strikes up, and we in the chorus stir and move and start twirling our hats. A mangrove island turns drift to dance. It creates its own soil as it goes, rocking over the salt sea at random, rocking day and night and round the sun, rocking round the sun and out toward east of Hercules.

RESPONSE

1. "If survival is an art, then mangroves are artists of the beautiful." What aspects of mangroves as revealed in this essay support this contention?
2. With your group, select three sentences from "Sojourners" that reveal the truth of Dillard's statement, "There are floating islands on the planet; it amazes me."

EXTENSION

3. a) Visit a garden. It could be a large, public "botanical" garden or a private garden in your neighbourhood. Bring back to your class some record of the plants you saw: a prose description, photographs, drawings, or poems.
   b) Write a poem or a short lyrical piece entitled "Possibilities for Beauty" based on your experience.
4. Look up the meaning of the word "sojourner." Write a journal entry entitled "Sojourner."

Contents by Other Themes

Contents by Form

Author Index

Credits

Page 3   From *In Search of Our Mothers' Gardens* by Alice Walker. Copyright © 1983, by Alice Walker. Reprinted by permission of Harcourt, Brace, Jovanovich, Inc.

Page 12   From *All I Really Need to Know I Learned in Kindergarten* by Robert Fulghum. Copyright © 1986, 1988 by Robert Fulghum. Reprinted by permission of Random House, Inc.

Page 15   From *A Businessman's Letters to His Daughters* by G. Kingsley Ward. Used by permission of the Canadian publishers, McClelland & Stewart, Toronto.

Page 20   From *Free To Be . . . A Family* by Marlo Thomas & Friends. Copyright © 1987 by Free To Be Foundation, Inc. Used by permission of Bantam Books, a division of Bantam Doubleday, Dell Publishing Group. Abridged version reprinted from *MS* Magazine, December 1987.

Page 27   From *Glamour*, October 1987.

Page 31   From *Young and Modern (YM)* magazine, September 1987.

Page 37   From *Seventeen*, May 1988. Originally published as "Vile as Smoke." *The New York Times*, January 6, 1988. Copyright © 1988 by The New York Times Company. Reprinted by permission.

Page 40   From *We Are Still Married*. Copyright © Garrison Keillor, 1989. Reprinted by permission of Penguin Books Canada Limited.

Page 44   From *The Morningside Papers* by Peter Gzowski. Used by permission of the Canadian publishers, McClelland & Stewart, Toronto.

Page 47   From *Harrowsmith*, January-February 1989. Reprinted by permission.

Page 51   From *More Than Words Can Say*. McClelland and Stewart, 1990.

Page 57   From *Bridges Magazine*, September-October 1988. Published by P.J. Spratt & Associates Inc.

Page 62   From *Chatelaine*, April 1989. Reprinted by permission.

Page 67   From *MS* magazine, June 1989. Reprinted with permission of *MS* magazine. Copyright © 1989.

Page 73   Reprinted courtesy of Sports Illustrated from Dec. 25 1989 / Jan. 1 1990 issue. Copyright © 1989 / 1990 Time Inc. Magazine Co. "Greg LeMond's Greatest Race" by E.M. Swift. All rights reserved. Condensed from Sports Illustrated by Reader's Digest Canadian Edition, November 1990.

Page 79   From Canadian Geographic Dec. '90 / Jan. '91.

Page 82   From *More Than Words Can Say*. McClelland and Stewart, 1990. Reprinted with the permission of the author. Copyright © Sandra Birdsell.

Page 89   From *Listen* magazine, July 1990. Reprinted by permission.

Page 94   From *Inside Memory: Pages From a Writer's Workbook* by Timothy Findley. Copyright © 1990 by Pebble Productions Inc. Published by Harper Collins Publisher Ltd.

Page 97   From *The Globe and Mail*, October 29, 1990. Reprinted by permission of the author, a contributor to *The Globe and Mail*, as well as Canadian and US magazines.

Page 101   From *The Solace of Open Spaces* by Gretel Ehrlich. Copyright © 1985 by Gretel Ehrlich. Used by permission of Viking Penguin, a division of Penguin Books USA Inc.

Page 105   From *The Globe and Mail*. Reprinted by permission.

Page 108   From *No Kidding*, by Myrna Kostash. Used by permission of the Canadian publishers, McClelland & Stewart, Toronto.

Page 116   From *The Globe and Mail*, December 6, 1990. Reprinted by permission.

Page 123   Excerpted from *Our Sustainable Table*, copyright © 1990 by the *Journal of Gastronomy*. Published by North Point Press and reprinted by permission.

Page 129   From *Bridges Magazine*, March 1988. Published by P.J. Spratt & Associates Inc.

Page 132   From *Inventing the Future*, by David Suzuki. Copyright © 1989 by David Suzuki. Reprinted with author's permission.

Page 136   Reprinted from *Alternatives*, Faculty of Environmental Studies, University of Waterloo, Ontario N2L 3G1

Page 142   From *A Hot Eyed Moderate* by Jane Rule. Lester and Orpen Dennys. Copyright © by Jane Rule 1986.

Page 146   From *Stalking the Wild Asparagus* by Euell Gibbons. Copyright © 1962, used by permission of Alan C. Hood and Company Inc., Brattleboro, Vermont.

Page 153   From *Canadian Geographic*, April/May 1989. Reprinted by permission of David Phillips, Senior Climatologist, Environment Canada.

Page 157   From *Will the Bounty End? The Uncertain Future of Canada's Food Supply*, by Garry Lawrence Fairbairn. Published by Western Producer Prairie Books. Copyright © 1984 by Garry Lawrence Fairbairn.

Page 160   From *Canadian Geographic*, June/July 1990. Reprinted by permission of David Phillips, Senior Climatologist, Environment Canada.

Page 164   From *The Book of Small*, by Emily Carr. Copyright © 1942 Oxford University Press. Reproduced with the permission of Stoddart Publishing Co. Limited, 34 Lesmill Rd., Don Mills, Ontario, Canada.

Page 167   From *Canadian Geographic*, February/March 1989.

Page 175   From *The Science of Everyday Life* by Jay Ingram. Copyright © Jay Ingram, 1989. Reprinted by permission of Penguin Books Canada Limited.

Page 183   Permission granted by the Albert Einstein Archives, The Hebrew University of Jerusalem, Israel.

Page 188   From *The Globe and Mail*, April 23, 1988. Reprinted with author's permission.

Page 193   From *Saturday Night*, July/August 1990.

Page 196   From *Nature Canada*, Fall 1987. Copyright © Christie McLaren.

Page 205   From *Teaching a Stone to Talk*, by Annie Dillard. Copyright © 1982 by Annie Dillard. Reprinted by permission of Harper Collins Publishers.

Every reasonable effort has been made to find copyright holders of the above material. The publishers would be pleased to have any errors or omissions brought to their attention.